WOMEN FROM AFGHANISTAN IN DIASPORA

Their Stories of Adversity, Freedom, and Success

Sayid Sattar Langary

authorHOUSE®

AuthorHouse™
1663 Liberty Drive
Bloomington, IN 47403
www.authorhouse.com
Phone: 1-800-839-8640

First published by AuthorHouse 6/3/2010

ISBN: 978-1-4520-2277-2 (e)
ISBN: 978-1-4520-2275-8 (sc)
ISBN: 978-1-4520-2276-5 (hc)

Library of Congress Control Number: 2010907163

Printed in the United States of America
Bloomington, Indiana

This book is printed on acid-free paper.

ABSTRACT

This exploratory study is a case study of eight adult Afghan women who migrated to the United States by means of marriage to Afghan American men. The study is based on qualitative research methods and in-depth face-to-face interviews. The women describe their immigration experience in the United States. The purpose of this study was to explore the thriving mail-order bride industry and how women as mail-order brides are represented. Based on a feminist theoretical lens and case study approach, the research addressed the questions whether traditional Afghan marriages were subjected to patriarchal norms and whether they impacted marriages among Afghan immigrants in California. The study also focused on the Afghan women's narratives, which showed that most of these women have found comfortable and economically stable lives. The participants did not, however, mention any type of subjugation, control, abuse, and domination by their husbands.

TABLE OF CONTENTS

Chapter 3

Chapter 4

Chapter 5

PREFACE

There were many reasons why I chose to write about Afghan women. First of all, Afghan women have always been victimized in so many ways by so many regimes. The theocratic regimes in Afghanistan along with some radical reformists particularly in the last century have mostly tried to target women. Women's rights have been one of the major reasons of conflict between the modernists, and the traditionalists, and fundamentalists throughout history. Today too, the international community and as well the Afghan modernists would like to establish gender equality, democracy, and human rights principles in Afghanistan. However, those of the traditionalists have been trying to reinforce religious traditions in every aspect of Afghan social life. They try to define the role of women and their freedom based on Islamic and non-Islamic traditions that have remained in Afghanistan for decades and even centuries.

My interest in social sciences in general has been due to my being an eyewitness of atrocity, inequality, and a victim of war since my childhood. Spending years of adversity and war during the Soviet occupation of Afghanistan and later during the bloody civil war by the Mujahideen, and later the Taliban in 1990s, made life unbearable in Afghanistan. From 1996 to 2002, life as a refugee in the neighboring country of Pakistan was one of the most challenging parts of life for both me and my family.

Witnessing refugee life in two major cities in Pakistan, Quetta and Peshawar, and working with Human Rights Watch and United Nations High Commissioner for Refugees, was the wakening phase of life for me. Interviews with Afghan refugees, particularly with the Afghan women, was the most heartbreaking while working with Human Rights Watch. Hearing their bitter experiences from life in Afghanistan during the war crises and under the brutal gender regime of the Taliban, I always raised questions about why things were as such. My experience working at the UNHCR, and hearing the refugees' stories of sufferings at refugee camps and other cities of Pakistan in the years of war, was even more of an awakening phase in my life.

After the tragedies of September 11th, 2001, the military intervention of the United States in Afghanistan, and the fall of the Taliban regime, tens of thousands of Afghan refugees began pouring back into Afghanistan through UNHCR on a daily basis. Refugees going back to Afghanistan through the UNHCR refugee voluntary repatriation project in Pakistan and Iran were igniting the light of hope in the Afghan people's hearts once again. People seeing an end to the despotic regime of the Taliban decided to move back to their homeland. My family was one of the volunteer repatriates as well.

Returning to Afghanistan in 2002 after six years of life in refuge was an unforgettable moment in my life. The three decades of war and drought left almost nothing in Afghanistan. The city of Kabul looked like ruins. The streets were empty, and one could hardly see houses that people lived in. Particularly in the Western regions of Kabul close to Kabul University, very few people were visible on the roads. There were various non-governmental organizations such as ACTED, UNDP, UNHCR, and so forth that were donating food, money, as well as windows, doors, and ceiling bars to people to build their houses.

Since 2002, life has been changing in Afghanistan rapidly. The number of United Nations offices and non-governmental organizations has been growing day by day and it reached 1600 by the year 2006. More and more schools, roads, and people's houses are built on a daily basis. There are various institutions working for women, as well as the Ministry of Women's Affairs in Afghanistan that has been working on advocacy programs for Afghan women. Over six and a half million children go to schools and universities and 42% of them are female students this year in 2009. Women are back to work in both government and non-government institutions.

After graduating from Kabul University in December of 2006 with a Bachelor of Arts degree in sociology, my life took a different course. Getting a Fulbright Scholarship for a Master's of Arts in Sociology at California State University Fullerton (CSUF) and moving to United States changed my life perspective. My educational goals moved my academic interests toward sociology, democracy, human rights, and gender studies. My personal experiences, goals in life, and also encouragement of my wonderful professors at California State University, Fullerton, led me toward writing this thesis about Afghan women.

ACKNOWLEDGMENTS

First of all, I want to express my sincere gratitude to my committee chair, Dr. Joseph Weber, for his patience and assistance with the proposal, IRB forms, interviews, and finally completion of the thesis. Dr. Weber was always available to meet with me, guide and motivate me, and discuss each sentence of my thesis. I am also grateful to my professors who were on my thesis committee, Dr. Jorge Fontdevila, and Dr. Carter Rakovski. They guided and motivated me to finish my thesis on time.

Most of all, I want to thank my congenial research participants—the eight Afghan women who opened their hearts and shared their life experiences. In addition, I want to thank the Writing Center at California State University, Fullerton for providing a wonderful opportunity where I could have the early drafts of my thesis proofread. Special acknowledgement goes to my friends—Solaiman Fazel, Qais Faqiri, and Justin Cook for their always estimable encouragements and support, and who read and listened to my thesis.

Lastly, with love I thank my mother, Safia Mushref, and my father, Quyyum Langary, and all my family for their always encouragements and for imbedding the value of education in me since my childhood.

Dedicated to Dr. Joseph Weber

Chapter 1

INTRODUCTION

In this research, the experience of Afghan immigrant women in the United States is told in their own voices. The in-depth analysis of interviews with these women in the state of California focuses on their subjective experience of life in the United States. Through marriage these women were brought to the United States by the husbands. They openly discuss their life stories, whether their lives with Afghan American men have changed for the better with more freedom and economic stability, or whether these women experience subjugation.

The women discuss both the dilemmas they face in the host country of United States and the issues that have worked for the betterment of their lives. The women describe their marriage to their Afghan American male counterparts and discuss the reasons why they married their husbands. They also talk about the traditions and monetary issues that involved their marriages. In addition, these Afghan immigrant women discuss their families back in Afghanistan and their current families in the United States.

A Background on Afghanistan
and the Afghan Family

Afghanistan is a society that needs a tremendous amount of scientific study. Years of the Soviet occupation, the civil war under the Mujahideen factions, and the Taliban regime have almost entirely destroyed the country's infrastructure during the last three decades. None of the schools, universities, libraries, and almost none of the buildings including residential apartments were left untouched by bullets and fire. Millions of people left the country and tens of thousands were killed. The turmoil under the Communist era and later the Civil War and the Taliban regimes took the country to the middle ages.

Particularly in regards to the Afghan people and culture, very few scientific articles have been written. Most of what was written about Afghanistan by Afghans no longer exists because most of the country's cultural heritage, including books and writings of scholars, were burned and destroyed. About almost every aspect of the Afghan society, non-Afghans, particularly the British, have written most of the books and articles. Today most historians including Afghan historians quote particularly the British and the Russian scholars who have recorded Afghanistan's history and society.

Historically given its geostrategic location, Afghanistan was the crossroad of civilizations three thousand years ago. It connected Central Asia, China, the Indian subcontinent, Persia, and the Middle East through the Silk Road. It was called the *Jewel of the East* (Ghobar, 2002). The region was called Ariana/Aria until the name changed to Khorasan under the Persian Empire. In 1747 Ahmad Shah Durani named the current territory Afghanistan. In 1919, King Amanullah Khan regained the political independence of Afghanistan from the British.

Since its birth, the landlocked country of Afghanistan has remained a small canvas. It is about the size of France and the State of Texas in the United States (Dupree, 2002). About 86% of Afghanistan's land encompasses several high mountain ranges and deserts. Afghanistan has borders with China, Tajikistan, Uzbekistan, Turkmenistan, Iran, and

Pakistan. It has an estimated population of 25 million, most of them under the age of thirty (Dupree, 2002, p.977).

About 99% of the Afghans are Muslims (Dupree, 2002; Ghobar, 2002; Sadat, 2008). Also Hindus, Buddhists, Sikhs, Christians, and Jews have lived in Afghanistan for centuries. The people are comprised of various ethnic groups that include Pashtun, Tajik, Hazara, Uzbek, Turkman, Baloch, Aimaq, Pashayee, Qirghiz, Qezelbash, Nuristani, and others. There are over thirty languages spoken in Afghanistan, the largest of which are Persian (Farsi-Dari) and Pashto (Sadat, 2008). Each ethnic group and sub-ethnic group has its own traditions, culture, and social values. They also share common religious and traditional values with other ethnic groups. The family is one of the most important institutions for all Afghan people (Dupree, 2002).

Nancy Dupree and her family have spent almost a century in Afghanistan and she has written several books and articles about Afghanistan. Dupree (2002) describes the Afghan society as follows:

> Honor is the rock upon which social status rests and the family is the single most important institution in Afghan society. Individual honor, a positive pride in independence that comes from self-reliance, fulfillment of family obligations, respect for the elderly, respect for women, loyalty to colleagues and friends, tolerance for others, forthrightness, an abhorrence of fanaticism, and a dislike for ostentation, is a cultural quality most Afghans share. The position of women is central to these values. In this patriarchal society women are the standards by which morality is judged, and they carry the responsibility of passing on the values of the society to younger generations. Many of these values are implicit in the rules of etiquette which emphasize respect for elders and guests, such as always standing in welcome, exchanges of prescribed greetings, appropriate dress, and, above all, decorum and deportment, which are as crucial for males as for females. Many of the rules for proper behavior concern male–female relationships which require separate

protected living, working and entertaining spaces. (Dupree 2002, p. 278)

Family and marriage is the most important social institution in the Afghan society. Particularly after the Soviet occupation, the Communist era in Afghanistan along with the civil war during the Mujahideen and the Taliban regimes from 1992 to 2001, the institution of family was severely affected. Women in particular suffered the most under the Taliban regime. Marriage and family laws changed dramatically and less attention was paid to women. Tens of thousands of men, women and children were killed during these political regime changes. Thousands of women lost their husbands and many children were left as orphans. In addition, millions started to escape the country and become refugee in neighboring countries and around the world.

IMMIGRATION OF AFGHANS

Afghan immigration has a long history. The first large phase of immigration started during the occupation of Afghanistan by the Soviet Red Army in 1979 (Fazel, 2009; Sadat 2008). Millions of Afghans migrated to Pakistan, Iran, as well as India and Turkey. Some, particularly the rich and those from the royal family, immigrated to Europe, Canada, and to the United States of America. According to Fazel (2009), before 1978 only a couple hundred Afghans, mostly students, lived in the United States temporarily. After the Soviet occupation, almost all these students were granted political asylum. Most of these asylum seekers sponsored their families to come to the United States through the "family reunification program" (Fazel, 2009). A large number of these immigrants came through marriage to the Afghans who had already earned their American citizenship. Most of these Afghan refugees settled in the States of California, New York, Washington D.C., and Virginia (Fazel, 2009).

The second wave of Afghan immigration began when the bloody civil war broke out between the Mujahideen factions from 1992 to1996. After that, the Taliban regime from 1996 to 2001 forced millions of

Afghans to escape out of Afghanistan, particularly those of the religious and ethnic minorities. According to Sadat (2008), today around 250,000 Afghans live in Europe, particularly in Netherlands, Germany, and Russia. In the United States, the number of refugees has reached approximately 260,000. Also, about 40,000 Afghan immigrants live in Canada and 19,000 in Australia (Sadat, 2008, p.332).

Today although the Taliban are not in power, the migration and outpouring of Afghans is ongoing due to the Taliban insurgency, unemployment, and security issues (Fazel, 2009). The government of Afghan President Hamid Karzai, along with the American troops and NATO forces, has maintained security in Afghanistan to a large extent. However, there is still threat from the Taliban in rural areas outside of the capital. Government employees face threat as well, particularly the women. In addition, the economical hardship, war threat, and fear of torture and killings by the Taliban make people leave the country.

Some Afghans who have relatives in Europe, Australia, Canada, and in the United States try to seek help for their immigration too. Marriage to one of the American citizens, particularly to an Afghan American, is one of the easiest ways to seek immigration to the United States (Fazel, 2009). In case of marriage, traditions and religious, tribal, and familial connections are the conditions for immigration to a large extent. In addition, the bride price, divorce issues, and consanguineous marriages are largely influenced by religious traditions that the immigrants bring with them in host countries (Aseel, 2003; Dupree, 2002; Sadat, 2008; Wahab, 2005).

THE CURRENT STUDY

This study is about mail-order bride marriage practices, and the men and women who are involved in this type of marriage. The focus of the study is Afghan immigrant women in California who have been brought to the United States through marriage by Afghan American men. One of the goals of the study is to find out how these marriages compare to the general mail-order bride practice.

In the study, eight Afghan women from the state of California speak about their life experiences and marital life. The study includes two sections about Afghan women. The major part of the study is the first hand knowledge about Afghan immigrant women in their own words through in-depth interviews. The other part is a literature review of the previous studies about Afghanistan and Afghan women. The literature is basically a review of academic journal articles and books written in the last decade written by Afghan and non-Afghan academics.

The first section of the literature review is about the mail-order bride industry. It explains who mail-order brides are and from what countries they mostly immigrate to their host countries. It also describes how and why they immigrate to their host countries, particularly to the United States, Canada, Western European countries, and Australia. The literature discusses the mail-order bride companies and how they have become a thriving industry in the last century, particularly after the use of the internet. It describes the mail-order couples and their experiences as well as expectations from each other. It also describes the roles of the men and women involved in this type of practice. The literature tries to find out the types of abuse and whether it takes place in marriages of this type.

The second phase of the literature review is focused on women from Afghanistan. First, the literature talks about Afghan women who have immigrated to United States through marriage and who share similar experiences as mail-order brides in general do. It talks about the reasons of how and why these Afghan women choose to marry somebody, predominantly Afghan immigrant men, in their host countries. It also talks about gender roles in these types of marriages among Afghan immigrants. Second, the literature describes the traditional practices in Afghan marriages. It describes the patriarchal norms in the Afghan culture and how traditionalism and religion affect both the lives of Afghan men and women. The literature focuses on both religious and non-religious traditions and the Afghan family structure, including monetary issues, polygamy, endogamy, consanguinity, patriarchy, and gender roles in marriage arrangements.

Finally, the literature review discusses gender roles and the Afghan family structure and its reforms in the last century. It starts from King Amanullah Khan's (1919-1929) to the current regime under President Hamid Karzai. The literature focuses on reformations and Afghan women's rights under each regime and ruler. The literature focuses on two major steps of reformations, first during Amanullah Khan and second during the Communist regimes, and how their reformation policies failed. It spotlights each regime's attitude and regulations toward Afghan women. In fact, regarding both their freedom and suppression Afghan women have been the main target under the laws and regulations of each regime.

SIGNIFICANCE OF THE STUDY

Little study has been done about the Afghan society. The articles have mostly been descriptive works written mostly by non-Afghan writers and researchers. Few qualitative articles exist about Afghan women who speak out about their concerns and rights. There have been few articles written about Afghan women considering their own voices. Particularly Afghan women's rights and the family institution have always been neglected in Afghanistan.

Afghanistan is famous for having a patriarchal social structure. Women, shown in *Burqas* on Kabul streets, bring to the world attention that Afghan women suffer from control, inequality, abuse, and so forth. However, little has been said to give Afghan women the agency and opportunity to speak out for themselves and talk about their own rights and dilemmas.

A qualitative research and case study approach was the appropriate method to find out the answers to the research questions in this study because listening to these women's voices provided a reasonable understanding and interpretation of their experiences and life stories in America. The eight in-depth interviews were conducted with Afghan women who had come to the United States through marriage. These interviews allowed the researcher to listen to the voices and narratives of Afghan immigrant women in their own words.

This is an important study. First, it is a qualitative study about Afghan immigrant women. The qualitative study paves the way in order to understand these women's voices in their own words. The participants talk about their own experiences and life stories in relation to their male counterparts. Secondly, the study is a contribution to the body of literature concerning gender inequality, domination, and abuse of women in general and in particular, Afghan immigrant women in California. Not much research has been done about Afghan immigrant women in the United States.

PURPOSE OF THE STUDY

The first purpose of this study was the graduate school requirement for the researcher. This piece is a thesis for a master's degree from California State University, Fullerton. The researcher had a Bachelors of Arts in sociology from Kabul University and this thesis is for his master's in Sociology.

The main goal of the study is to explore the rationalizations of Afghan immigrant women who have migrated to the United States through marriage. This study will give a first hand knowledge about Afghan immigrant women in California and will be a great contribution to the existing literature. The main purpose of the research was to find the answers to the research questions.

RESEARCH QUESTIONS

The study tried to do the following:

1. Explore and describe the subjective experience of Afghan women who immigrated to the United States through marriage to Afghan immigrant men.
2. Explore how marital experiences of Afghan immigrant women in California compared to traditional Afghan marriages and whether their stories reinforced or negated the stories in the literature on mail-order brides.

3. Provide a clear vision of some facts about marriage traditions that exist among Afghans in general and in particular among women who immigrate to the United States through marriage.
4. Identify the dilemmas that Afghan immigrant women are facing in the United States and in their marriage to Afghan American men.
5. Examine the voices and narratives of these women in their own words and provide themes about whether they perceive subjugation or freedom or both.
6. Find out whether Afghan women have acculturated and adapted into American society socially and economically.
7. Contribute to the increasing body of knowledge and literature about the mail-order bride industry, Afghan family traditions, and Afghan immigrant women.

THEORETICAL AND CONCEPTUAL FRAMEWORK

The current study attempts to investigate eight Afghan women's cases that have immigrated to the United States through marriage. The research examines the voices and experiences of these Afghan women in California. The key sociological terms to be used about Afghan women in this study are gender inequality, domination, domestic exploitation, subordination, and economic dependence of women on men.

The feminist voice-centered method of analysis is used in order to focus on the interviews about the women's concerns and marriage to Afghan immigrant men in the United States. With this epistemological standpoint, the focus is on gender inequality and domination in marriage practice. The standpoint also draws attention to the oppression of women in society, the dependency on men, and how gender inequality is constructed. This method is centrally concerned with hearing the voices of those silenced, othered, and marginalized by the dominant social order (Babbie, 2006). This theory focuses on the position that women occupy within a social context characterized by a patriarchal sex-gender system (Hesse-Biber, 2005).

One of the theorists is Charlotte Perkins Gilman, who takes a rational approach in explaining gender inequality and women's economic dependence on men. In her *Women and Economics 1898*, she argues that the pre-existing social structure of traditional gendered division of labor is what makes women dependent on their male counterpart (Applerouth and Edles, 2008, p. 212). Gilman defines such gendered (over-sexed) dependency of women on men economically as "the natural tendency of any function to increase in power by use causes sex-activity to increase under the action of sexual selection" (*Women and Economics 1898 in* Applerouth and Edles, 2008, p. 225). She argues that although women are born physically capable as men, their sexual distinctions in society and how they grow up with such distinctions, makes them docile and weak. Gilman refers to women and states precisely that "what we do and what is done to us, makes what we are" (*Women and Economics 1898 in* Applerouth and Edles 2008, p. 209).

Moreover, according to Gilman, women are over-sexed and their pre-determined sexual attraction and activity is what makes them believe that "economic profit will only come through the power of sex-attraction" (*Women and Economics 1898 in* Applerouth and Edles, 2008, p. 226). Men have a lot of opportunities but women can achieve opportunities through over-sexed expectations, or "a small gold ring" (*Women and Economics 1898 in* Applerouth and Edles, 2008, p. 229) otherwise she will not have any economic status of any kind *Women and Economics 1898 in* Applerouth and Edles, 2008, p. 227). Thus, Gilman takes a Marxist approach and sets forth that women are like Marx's naive proletariat that live in false satisfaction and who have adapted to the oppressive condition of being economically dependent upon the male.

The integration of qualitative research and case study methods supported by a feminist epistemological point of view best suit this research. Through this method, the researcher was able to further analyze the interview data by attaching meaning and sociological significance to it and by explaining the patterns, categories, and relationships that emerged from the interviews. Therefore, this approach helped to evaluate the underlying meanings of traditional marriage practices by Afghan immigrants and the narratives of Afghan immigrant women in their own words.

Chapter 2

LITERATURE REVIEW

THE MAIL-ORDER BRIDE PHENOMENON

Many books, journal articles, and other resources are available about mail-order brides who immigrate from Russia, Eastern Europe, Southeast Asia, and South America. However, there are very few articles written about Afghan immigrant women and Afghan traditional marriage practices in the United States. Some of the resources include articles about the mail-order bride industry, and also the reasons why men and women practice this type of marriage. The review of the literature gives details on the relationship between the mail-order brides and their husbands. This literature review also explains whether these marriages work for women, and whether they find freedom, and economically stable lives. In short, the intent of this literature review is to situate this study in the context of other scholarly work.

The following literature is on mail-order brides and the mail-order bride industry. The focus will be on Afghan women in California who have immigrated through marriage. In addition, the literature will address the Afghan women and the Afghan family structures in the last century. Past studies describe the traditional marriages and gender roles in the Afghan society.

THE MAIL-ORDER BRIDE INDUSTRY

Traditionally, mail-order brides are women who immigrate from South America, Southeast Asia, Eastern Europe, and Central Asia through marriage. These women advertise their profiles in catalogues, newspapers, magazines, and websites in order to get married to the citizens of developed countries such as the United States, Western Europe, Australia, and Canada. With the emergence of the internet, the mail-order bride industry has transformed from regional to a global phenomenon. Some literature portrays the mail-order bride industry as enhancing emotional and physical abuse, domestic violence, and human trafficking of women (Eng, 2006; Lee, 2008). On the other hand, mail-order bride practice is often represented as an opportunity for freedom, economic stability, and immigration opportunity for women (Clark, 2004; Johnson, 2007). These include women from middle class families as well as those who come from impoverished backgrounds (Clark, 2004; Kojima 2001; Minervini and Francis, 2006). Currently, the mail-order bride companies have become a thriving industry.

The mail-order bride industry is more than a century old (Langevin and Belleau, 2000; Minervini and Francis, 2006). Prior to the 1990s, companies advertised these women in catalogs. In later 1990s, when the internet became widespread, mail-order bride businesses increased exponentially and became a thriving industry around the world. It became easier for men to find women and to establish contact with them through the Internet (Felicity-Schaeffer, 2006).

In order to grow further and find more customers, the mail-order bride companies carefully use labels such as "ladies" and "gentlemen" and discussions of "courtship" and "romance" rather than "sex" in order to make the language of marriage classier (Eng, 2006; Hochschild, 2002). The industry seeks to heighten the personal introductions of women by highlighting their youth, commitment, ambition, trustworthiness, and willingness to raise a family (Buss, 2001). They characterize these women in a way to show that they are feminine, obedient, family-oriented, committed, faithful, and even willing to marry middle-aged divorced men (Narayan, 2000).

Such characterization of mail-order brides typifies Western women as too assertive and spoiled by feminism and justifies the practice of mail-order marriages by Western men. Such characterization of Western family values, Western women, and feminism can subordinate women further by misrepresenting the social life in the Western world. It can also encourage men to further seek mail-order bride services. The industry uses various techniques in order to gain more members and encourage men to seek brides from them.

MAIL-ORDER EXPECTATIONS

Some researchers found that mail-order brides look for educated, ambitious, faithful, and healthy men who are also willing to have children (Minervini and Francis, 2006). In order to attract men, these women show less interest in attractiveness, and political and religious views of their potential husbands. The women also perceive Western men as more egalitarian partners who will give them an enjoyable life, more freedom, and who value their contributions and commitments to the home and family (Felicity-Schaeffer, 2006). Hence, some of these women want to marry men in developed countries in hope of a better lifestyle, more freedom, and establishing a family regardless of the men's age or attractiveness, or their religious and political affiliations.

According to Felicity-Schaeffer (2005), gender equality in the Western world encourages men to seek mail-order brides who are less feminist. He found that "some White American male participants wanted a less liberated, less spoiled and less materialistic woman. They also thought 'feminazis' create gender and sexual disorder within the family and nation" (Felicity-Schaeffer, 2005, p. 340). In addition, Hooper (2001) asserts that some men think they have lost authority in the family and that is why they desire to marry mail-order brides. These studies show that men want women who are obedient to them. Putting the burden on feminism as the cause for gender and sexual disorder, these men try to legitimize their own interests in mail-order bride.

Minervini and Francis research (2006) focused on South American mail-order brides. The study showed that men constantly stated that they could find better, younger, and more beautiful women in Latin America than in the United States. They also believed that Latina women were more caring, warmer, more loving to their husbands, and more devoted to their family than White women. On the other hand, Latina women want White men because they perceive them as "more faithful, less jealous, and less chauvinistic" than Latino men (Minervini and Francis, 2006, p. 115). This is a very controversial issue and needs further elaboration on the participants' ages and how they perceive middle-aged American men as more "faithful, less jealous, and less chauvinistic" compared to Latino men.

MAIL-ORDER BRIDE EXPERIENCE

Multiple studies discuss the mail-order bride industry as oppressive, sexist, abusive, and subordinating toward women. In these studies, the mail-order brides repeatedly reported that they confront a broad range of men's abusive behaviors, including emotional, physical, domestic, and sexual exploitation, and financial control (Eng, 2006; Lee, 2008; Minervini and Francis, 2006). Anderson (1993) states that cultural and linguistic differences between couples might hinder communication, compassion, and understanding. She adds, "When these cross-cultural interchanges do result in marriage, unrealistic expectations on both sides often mean severe incompatibility at best, and outright abuse at worst" (Anderson, 1993, p. 1410).

If abuse takes place and the woman wants a divorce, her husband may threaten to send her back to her county (Anderson, 1993; Minervini and Francis, 2006; Narayan, 2000). Since these women are rarely aware of the host nation's laws, the fear of being deported makes them more vulnerable and defenseless. Therefore, their fear causes them to limit their alternatives to their relationships and become subject to further abuse and violence.

Some articles, however, discuss that some mail-order brides achieve their dreams. They are immigrating from destitute economical conditions, and are searching for a better environment abroad. These women immigrate abroad in order to find husbands and form families which they think are a privilege for them. They do not regard themselves as "victims" (Clark, 2004; Johnson, 2007). Some of these women do not even want to have children for a while. They spend some time with their husbands and may seek divorce once they obtain green cards or citizenship in host countries (Minervini and Francis, 2006).

Thus, mail-order bride practice is controversial in many ways. Some women find the marriage suitable in many ways. They find gender equality, freedom, and happiness with more egalitarian men. They also find economical stability and find jobs that make them self-sufficient and less dependent on their husbands. Nevertheless, some of these women find themselves victims that men take advantage of. They neither want to stay in an abusive relationship with men nor can they go back to where they came from for many reasons. The reasons could be suffering not only from violence but also from loneliness, depression, and, more importantly, fear of being sent back to her country (Minervini and Francis, 2006).

Afghan Mail-Order Brides

The traditional marriages that are practiced by some Afghan immigrants in the United States are similar to mail-order bride phenomenon in many different ways. Afghan men not only use the Internet and certain websites[1] in order to find Afghan female partners but they also contact families in Afghanistan, go there, marry and bring their brides to the United States. Before discussing the tradition of mail-order bride practice by Afghan immigrants, it is essential to shed some light on religion, traditions, and the Afghan family structures.

A Background on Religion, Traditions, and the Afghan Family Structure

The Afghan society is profoundly subjective to patriarchal norms and attitudes (Aseel, 2003; Dupree, 2002; Wahab, 2005). Religion and traditions play an important role in family structure and gender roles in the Afghan family. In spite of some socio-political struggles and reforms by some rulers in the last century, the family institution has remained traditional. Religiosity mixed with traditionalism has had a major influence on almost every aspect of Afghan people's lives, particularly on marriage and family structures.

In the Afghan culture, marriage is very much structured by religion and traditions (Aseel, 2003; Dupree, 2002, Wahab, 2005). Marriage is considered a religious duty for both men and women. Most Afghan men and women get married at a young age because delay in marriage is considered religiously inappropriate. Those who live in rural areas in particular should get married when they can afford marriage financially and health wise (Dupree, 2002). Moreover, families continue to practice

---

1   [1] Some of the major websites that Afghan men and women use for dating/marriage are http://afghansingles.com, www.afghanperonals.com, http://afghansite.com, http://afgsingles.com, http://afghanmatch.com/ , http://af.singlescrowd.com/, and so forth.

dowry, and endogamous, consanguineous and occasionally polygamous marriages (Dupree, 2002; Wahab 2005).

Family and social bonds are very strong in Afghanistan. These bonds are strongly tied by familial, religious, and tribal traditions. In both urban and rural areas, engagements, weddings, birthday parties,[2] funerals, *Eid,*[3] *Nawroz,*[4] and so forth are all social occasions that "provide significant bonding experiences" in extended families (Dupree, 2002, p. 312).

Typically, about three generations at least live together in Afghan families (Dupree, 2002). Grandparents are highly respected. Fathers and grandfathers are the main patriarchs in the family and they expect obedience from children. Both grandparents and parents show affection to their children. They preach social values, manners, and often tell stories and oral history to their children and grandchildren. Everybody treats mothers with profound affection. In return, the care and protection of parents in their old age is considered a major duty of the children (Dupree, p. 312).

According to Dupree (2002) extended families play an essential role in the Afghan society. She believes the extended family functions as "the major economic, social, and political unit of the society and guarantees security, from birth to death, to each man and woman. It is the central focus where individuals find status, socialization, education, economic security, and protection" (Dupree, 2002, p. 313). The head of the household is generally the patriarch who is the grandfather

---

2   It is not common for Afghans to celebrate Birth Day parties every year. However, the day the son or daughter is born, families celebrate the birth of the child by inviting the musicians, family, and relatives, and sometimes by fireworks and gun fire.

3   Eid is a religious celebration and a public holiday. There are two Eids. The first one is after the month of Ramadan and is called Eid-e-Ramadan. The second Eid is two months after Eid-e-Ramadan and is called Eid-e-Qurban. Both days are celebrated 3-4 days all over Afghanistan.

4   Nawroz is 21st of March. It is the first day of the Solar year. It is celebrated all over Afghanistan and it is a public holiday that is inherited from Zoroastrians.

and father. In the absence of grandfather or father, the eldest son is the decision maker and leader. The patriarch makes almost all the decisions at home, such as economic and financial decisions, family meetings, engagements and weddings, funerals, and so forth. Also the father or grandfather, the patriarch, approves marriage of his sons, daughters, and grandchildren (Dupree, 2002).

The patriarch and sometimes the women in the family organize weddings and marriages. The decision about the marriage of their son to a girl from a family or tribe is almost always made by the father and mother in the family. Both couples try to fulfill the happiness of their children. They want to find the best partner for their children. However, sometimes there is disagreement between the couple about the choice of daughter-in-law or son-in-law. In such cases, usually the man's decision prevails.

Often the disagreement is about their son or daughter's marriage to one of the party's family members. The mother tries to find a girl or a boy from her family, usually her niece and nephews. The father tries to get his nephews and nieces or even distant family members. When parents have proposals for their daughter, they usually agree when the boy is rich, educated, and healthy (Dupree, 2002). In addition, particularly during the last three decades, some families prefer when the man is a citizen of one of the Western countries. In addition, most of the time the parents agree when the bride is the best choice and when the arrangement does not cost much.

Dowry—a large bride price under various names such as *mahr*,[5] *shirbaha*,[6] *gala*,[7] *walwar*,[8] or *toyana*—is a common practice among a large number of people in Afghanistan, particularly those in rural areas. Also *jawab-e-shirini* is an additional amount of money that the groom's family pays to his own will when they get a "yes" answer or *shirini* for the proposal. In addition to cash, some marriages are also linked with material exchanges of land and herds as part of the dowry. Although some people practice dowry in a religious way as *mahr*, many people ask for a large bride price unrelated to religion which men often cannot afford (Aseel, 2003, p. 129). Some of the money goes to the family and some of it is spent for the brides' *jez*[9] when she leaves her parents' home. Sometimes men find it harder to marry a bride from a different tribe.

When men propose to a bride from another tribe, they usually should either give a high bride price or exchange a woman from their tribe as a bride to the other tribe in return (Wahab, 2005; Barrenburg, 2003). Thus, a bride from one tribe costs another bride from the proposing tribe.

---

5 *Mahr* is monetary or material gift, mandatory in Islam, given by the groom to the bride upon marriage. It is considered to be a form of appreciation, as well as providing certain guarantees for the woman. It may be paid in cash, property, or movable objects to the bride herself. The amount of *mahr* is not legally specified; however, moderation according to the existing social norm is recommended. The *mahr* may be paid immediately to the bride at the time of marriage, or deferred to a later date, or a combination of both. The deferred *mahr*, however, falls due in case of death or divorce (Wikipedia.com)

6 [6] *Shirbaha* is the price and value of milk that the bride's mother fed her when she was an infant. This money generally goes to the bride's mother. It is not a religious practice like *Mahr*.

7 *Gala* is the price of the girl. The amount of gala depends on tribe and families. It starts from 200,000 Afghanis (equivalent to $4000) to 500,000 Afghanis ($10,000).

8 *Walwar* is similar to *Gala*.

9 *Jez* is the equipment and material that the bride's family gives to their daughter as gift when she leaves home after marriage. *Jez* includes materials such as carpets, bride's clothes, washing machine, sewing machine, kitchen equipment, fans, TVs, DVD player or VCR, and so forth.

However, the most common types of marriages are the consanguineous marriages and there is less worry about the price of the bride.

Most often in consanguineous marriages, there is no bride price involved as *toyana, shirbaha, gala,* or *walwar.* Marriage with the father's brother's daughter or the mother's brother's daughter is very common. In addition, the father's sister's daughter and the mother's sister's daughter are pretty common too. These first cousin as well as second cousin marriages are very simple and there is "no need to give or take" (Wahab, 2005, p. 320). The families do not worry about the finances and the couple because the families already know each other and share the same family blood. *Mahr,* however, is a religious concept and it remains intact.

The women usually do the marriage brokering and *khastgari.*[10] During *khastgari,* the sisters, mother, grandmother, aunts, and sisters-in-law introduce themselves and the man to the bride's family if they are from a distant family or tribe. Usually the to-be groom is not present during *khastgari* and the women bring a photo of him with them to the bride's family. They describe the best they can about their son's skills, job, education, habits, and manners. The girl's family members also reiterate and admire their daughter's beauty, manners, hardworking, and sometimes education, and so forth.

Usually, *khastgari* is not finalized in one session. In the case of a disagreement and too many demands from the bride's family, the marriage proposal could go null and void in the very first or second rounds of *khastgari.* In some instances, marriages do not happen because of tribal, ethnic, linguistic, political, and religious considerations and differences. In addition, the bride may come from a liberal family and the man's family might be conservative. The groom's family might demand that after marriage the bride should stay home and take care of the children and not work outside of home. They might even stipulate that their daughter wear *chadari / burqa* when she goes out of the house.

---

10   *Khastgari* is the official proposal of a girl from her family. Usually *Khastgari* happens when women go and talk to the bride's family first and in the second step, usually the father along with the grandfather of the son goes to the bride's family in order to propose the daughter for their son.

Sometimes families even demand that the girl should quit school after marriage. Some families might agree to such conditions and some do not. The marriage decisions are usually made when there are commonalities between the two families.

Women from the man's family visit the bride's family and usually get *lafz/balay* ("Yes" answer) in 3rd, 4th, or even 5th *khastgari* sessions. Families usually say "No" in the first round. However, if there were some commonalities between the families, they will take it easy after the first or second *khastgari*. If they come to an agreement, both fathers and mothers and occasionally grandparents negotiate the expenses with the family of the bride. Here, each party tries their best for their benefit.

MARRIAGE COSTS AND EXPENSES

Usually, the families try to bargain and negotiate the *mahr, shirbaha, gala, walwar,* and *toyana*. They talk about the engagement and wedding expenses. The issue regarding where the engagement and wedding should be celebrated, the number of guests to be invited, and the food that should be served, is also discussed during *khastgari*. Particularly among families in urban areas, although some may not ask for a bride price, usually the bride's family prefers that the wedding be held in a wedding hall. The number of guests in a wedding ceremony starts from a list of 200 (from each host family) to even 1000. The reception costs can go from $5,000 to $30,000. Thus, these are important issues that both parties talk about before a final decision. In rural areas, however, people celebrate the engagement and weddings in their houses. They usually use their close neighbors' houses for guests which brings costs down to a large extent compared to wedding halls.

Other costs include the musical band and singers for the wedding, bride's jewelry, bride's dresses, the *sufra*,[11] the photography and filming, and the "decorated vehicle"[12] in a florid style for the bride and groom.

---

11   Sufra is decoration of the bride and groom's sofa, with traditional food, cake, and drinks to be served during Nekah and Wedding in a wedding hall.

12   In Afghanistan, traditionally vehicles are decorated with flowers

Families also negotiate what kind of jewelry they want for the bride. The jewelry includes the gold rings, bracelets, necklace, and occasionally a gold crown and a golden belt. This set of jewelry could cost from $2,000 to $10,000.

These back-breaking expenses cost the man's family a fortune. Usually the men save for years to provide such demands to the bride's family. Sometimes, they even borrow money from friends or relatives. They also sometimes sell or rent their cars, a piece of land, and some of their herd in order to provide the money for the wedding. Many cannot get married even until their middle and old ages because they cannot afford it. Some finally marry a woman who costs less and whom they do not really want.

Here, consanguineous marriages are a great help for men to find their brides easily. It also costs less because guests will only be from among their own relatives and tribe. Once they get married, divorce and separation in later life become rare (Dupree, 2002). In addition to divorce, the consanguineous marriages also protect the bride from an *ambaq*[13] entering her life.

MARRIAGE ARRANGEMENTS

Divorce is not common in Afghanistan. It is "rarely contemplated, much less concluded . . . and it is the cause of much shame" (Dupree, 2002, p. 313). When the couple gets divorced, the wife is sent back to her parent's home. In addition, the divorced woman never marries again, and the widow, too, often stays with her family or with one of their brothers (Dupree, 2002). There should be a strong excuse for divorce. Women rarely initiate the divorce. The major factor for a woman asking for divorce could be extreme family violence or when the man marries a second wife and makes it unbearable for her.

Polygyny occurs occasionally and for various reasons. It is allowed in the religion of Islam to marry more than one woman under certain

---

when used to transport the bride and groom.

13   *Ambaq* is the second or third wife of a woman's husband.

conditions.[14] However, regardless of what Islam says, a man traditionally marries a second or a third wife just because he is rich, and he wants to have another wife. Also, a second wife comes when the first wife is not fertile. Marrying a second wife also happens because the wife has daughters but not sons. Fertility has been a measure of a woman's "prestige" and according to Dupree childlessness is a "disaster" and causes much anguish and distress (Dupree, 2002, p. 322).

Almost always, the wife is blamed and the husband, who might be responsible for the infertility, is not recognized as such. In addition to overcoming barrenness, the reasons for marrying a second wife are "to secure sons, to provide security for spinsters, and to cement political and social ties" (Dupree, 2002, p. 313). Nonetheless, the first two reasons seem more prevalent in today's Afghan society.

Many traditionally prefer sons to daughters. When the son gets married, he brings home a bride that will contribute to both domestic and out-of-home activities (Dupree 2002). Sons mostly stay with their families when they get married; however, daughters leave home and move to their husbands' homes. In this patriarchal structure, the daughter is a "guest" in her parents' house. When she leaves her home, she starts her new life. She moves to her husband's home, and with her, all decisions pertaining to her rights and duties are transferred to the family of her husband, (Dupree, 2002, p. 313).

Rural and urban Afghanistan is different in terms of how traditional and religious people are. In rural and urban areas the gender roles vary. In both urban and rural regions women do exercise considerable influence in "domestic management, nurturing, child socialization, community network activities, information dissemination, and marriage brokering, a role carrying wide-ranging influence" (Dupree, 2002, p. 313). There are stereotypes about rural women as "ignorant chattel

---

14   Islam allows a man to marry more than one on certain conditions. The Quran verse 3 of Surat Al Nisa says: "If ye fear that ye shall not be able to deal justly with the orphans, marry women of your choice, two, or three, or four; but if ye fear that ye shall not be able to deal justly (with them), then only one ..."

with no egos," used for the purposes of drudgery, reproduction, and sexual pleasure (Dupree, 2002, p. 313). In reality, Dupree believes that although labor is gender-based in rural areas, women play a significant role in the economy, particularly in handicrafts. Women in urban areas are less self-assured and largely confined to domestic work with more restrictions (Dupree, 2002). Hence, a more detailed study is needed to find out more about urban and rural Afghan women.

In short, religion, traditions, and patriarchy have had a major impact on family structures in Afghanistan. The practice of dowry and endogamous, consanguineous, and polygamous structures of families are influenced by religious traditions and have made social bonds very strong among Afghan extended families. Dowry, which is commonly practiced particularly by people in rural areas, is asked by the bride's family under various titles. In consanguineous marriages, there is less worry about the bride price. In addition to unaffordable bride prices, men find it hard to marry outside their own clan, tribe, ethnic group, or into families with different ideology, religious belief, language, and political opinion. These are possible reasons that people usually prefer consanguineous marriages. Polygamous marriages and divorce are also more unlikely to happen in consanguineous marriages. It also occurs when women are expected to be fertile and have male children (without men considering their own fertility) but she has no children or she has only daughters. Thus, these traditions have existed in the Afghan society for decades and even centuries despite the struggles for reformation by some.

MARRIAGE LAWS AND REFORMS DURING THE LAST CENTURY

Afghan Women

Political and social changes in the last century have always brought women to the center of attention. Each regime change has had its own laws and regulations for women's education, marriage, employment, empowerment, and other freedom related issues. It is important to mention that President Hamid Karzai has been the only president that was freely elected by the people of Afghanistan in 2004. The previous rulers and regimes were not based on elections; they were either monarchs, or those who gained power through coup d'etat, or somehow gained power and ruled. The following summary of literature includes the policies of rulers or leaders towards modernization and reform of women's rights starting from King Amanullah Khan (1919-1929) and finishing with the current President of Afghanistan, Hamid Karzai.

King Amanullah Khan (1919-1929) was the first Afghan king who took extensive steps towards Afghanistan's modernization since its birth in the eighteenth century (Dupree, 2002; Ghobar 2002; Sadat, 2008). According to Ghobar (2001) Amanullah Khan, influenced by Mahmood Tarzi, his father-in-law and foreign minister, traveled out of the country and brought some new ideas of modernization and development. He introduced his *Nizam Namah* (constitution), the first constitution of Afghanistan. His reforms included "government licensing requirements for clerics and religious judges, identification cards, taxation, conscription and draft requirements, emancipation of women, and compulsory [secular] education" for both men and women (Dupree, 2002, p. 314). He proclaimed his intention to extensively involve women in nation building. Queen Suraya, and the wives of Amanullah's cabinet appeared unveiled publicly during the Independence Day. All women were allowed to remove their veil voluntarily (Dupree, 2002, p. 314). Amanullah outlawed child marriage, and gave women the right to choose their husbands. He also restricted the laws for wedding expenses, *mahr,* and the bride price (Dupree, 2002; Saddat, 2008).

King Amanullah Khan

Amanullah Khan established *Anjoman-i-Hemayat-I Neswan* (The Association for the Protection of Women's Rights) to empower women and help them in order to fight "domestic injustice" (Dupree, 2002; Moghadam, 2002, p. 21). He, along with his wife Queen Soyara, founded *Ershad-e Niswan,* a popular magazine for women, and opened the first girls' school named Essmat Lycee in 1921. The king sent girls to study in Turkey, Switzerland, France, and other countries (Moghadam,

2002). He proposed to reform family laws and other issues concerning women, which became the center of debate in the *Loya Jirga Milli* (Grand National Assembly) of 1924.

Amanullah Khan audaciously wanted to outlaw polygamy. He defended this reform by citing the Quranic verse 3 of *Surat-al-Nisa* which states that "if ye fear that ye shall not be able to deal justly with the orphans, marry women of your choice, two, or three, or four; but if ye fear that ye shall not be able to deal justly (with them), then only one." Also, Amanullah Khan argued that "dealing justly with all of one's wives is humanly very difficult if not impossible, and therefore, polygamy should be established as unlawful." Article 18 of his *Nizam Namah* prohibited forced marriage men from forcing a widow to remain unmarried for the rest of her life (Dupree, 2002, p. 393). In addition, Amanullah banned slavery and discrimination and took firm steps toward the secularization of Afghanistan. Moghadam further states:

> By the late 1920s, Afghan legislation pertaining to women and the family was among the most progressive in the Muslim world. No other country had yet addressed the sensitive issues of child marriage and polygamy. Afghan family law on these issues became the model for similar reforms in Soviet Central Asia in 1926. (Moghadam, 2002, p. 20)

Clerics and other traditionalist tribal leaders, on the other hand, were incensed and argued intensely against his proposals and decrees on polygamy, divorce, *mahr*, and the legal age for marriage. The king was denounced as *kafi*, and "the enemy of faith" and he was ousted from power and exiled to Italy (Dupree, 2002; Sadat, 2008; Moghadam, 2002). Traditionalism and tribalism played its role as a severe obstacle for Amanullah's reform actions. People were not ready for his modern thoughts and therefore his government led to failures and anarchy.

After Amanullah was exiled, the unrest brought to power Habibullah Kalakani, known as *Bache-e-Saqaw* (the son of the water carrier), an illiterate man influenced by clerics and tribal leaders (Dupree, 2002; Moghadam, 2002, p. 21). For nine months (Jan 1929 to Oct 1929) he ran a weak government and did not accomplish almost anything. He did not have any development plans. After nine months, Kalakani was executed by General Mohammad Nadir who had returned from France to assume the throne of Amanullah (Fazel, 2008; Moghadam 2002).

Nadir Shah (1930-1933) denounced certain reformations by Amanullah. He closed secular schools, including schools for girls. He replaced secular courts with Shariya courts and founded a religious constitution for Afghanistan. In addition, he made it compulsory that women wear the *burqa* (Moghadam, 2002). Three years later he was assassinated, and his son, Zahir Shah, inherited his thrown at the age of nineteen.

Zahir Shah (1933–1973) was declared as King. His policies, however, were majorly influenced by his uncles, since he was a teenager and inexperienced. In his 1964 constitution, Zahir Shah declared that no provisions be hideous to Islam. Nevertheless, he changed some of his father's policies regarding women. He reopened schools for girls and declared that women have "the right to free education, freedom of choice in marriage and employment, and equality in the workplace" (Moghadam, 2002, p. 21). Particularly in the last decade of his monarchy, a large number of Afghan girls joined schools and universities. Kabul University became co-educational in 1960. Many women did not wear the *burqa* anymore and they enjoyed some basic freedoms.

In 1965, while Zahir Shah was still in power, the People's Democratic Party of Afghanistan (PDPA), backed by the Soviet Union, was formed by some Afghans who wanted to re-establish some of the reformation laws proposed by Amanullah Khan to "rescue Afghanistan from backwardness" (Dupree, 2002). Also in the same year, the Democratic Organization of Afghan Women was established by the PDPA. The goal of the organization was to "eliminate illiteracy among women, forced marriages, and the bride-price" (Moghadam, 2002, p. 22). Both these organizations wanted to bring insightful, extensive, and enduring social change. However, conservatives in the parliament protested. They outlawed female education abroad and women with western dresses in public, especially teachers and students. This resulted in demonstration by thousands of women in Kabul (Moghadam, 2002, p. 22).

Zahir Shah had gone to Italy in 1973 for an eye surgery when his cousin and the Prime Minister, Sardar Mohammad Daud Khan (1973–978), gained power through a coup d'état and established the Republic of Afghanistan. After about thirty years, Zahir Shah returned to Afghanistan in June 2002 and died in July of 2007 from severe illness. Daud Khan ended the monarchy in Afghanistan. He did not proclaim himself as a king, but rather the first President of Afghanistan.

Daud Khan initiated a ten-year modernization plan. The Marriage Law of 1977 by Daud Khan once again tried to reform marriage law. It banned child marriage and set the age of 16 as a minimum age of marriage for girls. It did not, however, reform divorce laws. The wife could not divorce the husband (Moghadam, 2002). Although men were predominantly the decision makers in the patriarchal natured Afghan society, Afghan women worked and went to school (Moghadam, 2002).

The PDPA came to power with a coup d'etat on April 27 of 1978. Daud Khan and most of his family were murdered by the PDPA in the Presidential Palace in Afghanistan. Noor Muhammad Taraki (1978-1979) was declared as President and he established the Democratic Republic of Afghanistan (DRA), also know as the *Saur* (April) Revolution. The party intended to reform Afghanistan and bring change in the social and political structure of society. Over 600 schools were established for both girls and boys. Decree No. 7 banned the payment of the dowry and bride price and gave women the freedom to choose their husband. Once again the women's age of 16 and men's age of 18 were set as minimums for marriage. Women could once again have the right to divorce. The DRA also regulated compulsory literacy classes for both men and women. Women were asked to be more involved with the formulation of laws and national policies (Dupree, 2002).

The regime revised the academic curriculum of schools and universities and added the Marxist ideology in the educational system. Girls and boys were sent to the Soviet Union for higher education. According to Dupree, about two thousand students participated in foreign exchange every year "willingly or unwillingly." Decree No.7 outlawed the bride-price. It also prohibited child marriage, forced marriage, bride price (cash and commodity), and levirate marriages. People thought all these reforms were interfering with the people's religious values and traditions. Hatred in the people's hearts was growing everyday. This resulted in tribal leaders and clerics rising up against the DRA (Dupree, 2002; Moghadam, 2002).

The turmoil caused the country to go to war between the modernists and the traditionalists. As a consequence, Taraki was killed by Hafizullah Amin (September-December 1979). In December 1979 the Soviet army intervened and backed the DRA. Hafizullah Amin was killed by the Soviets. Babrak Karmal (1980-1986) succeeded Amin and gained power, also known as *Marhala-e-Dowom* (the second phase). The people's struggle and war continued; Karmal was replaced in 1986 by Dr. Najibullah (1986-1992). In 1989 the Soviets pulled out of Afghanistan (Moghadam, 2002).

The Mujahideen, the so called guardians of Islam, "influenced by the Egyptian *Ikhwan ul-Muslimin*, the Muslim Brotherhood, and Pakistan's religious/political *Jamaat-i-Islami* party" were determined to change the Afghan society and establish a Islamic government. The Mujahideen thought of Dr. Najib's government as a Soviet puppet and part of the PDPA and therefore did not recognize it as legitimate. They started their guerilla wars from the provinces of Afghanistan around Kabul and enervated Dr. Najib's government day by day. The DRA government was only confined to Kabul. Thus, the Mujahideen collapsed Dr. Najib's government in 1992 (Moghadam, 2002). Dr. Najibullah sought asylum at the United Nations office in Kabul until 1996 when the Taliban removed him from United Nation's office in Kabul and hanged him and his brother in public.

Once the Mujahideen took power, Sebghatullah Mujadidi became the first interim president for two months. Then, Burhanuddin Rabbani started his two month term but stayed in power because the implacable civil war broke out between the Mujahideen[15] factions. They disagreed

---

15   Mujahideen were basically seven political parties all of whom had one agenda which was the holy war against the Soviets and over throw of the communist regime. However, civil war among the Mujahideen in Afghanistan was based on race, religious sect, ethnic, and linguistic considerations.

on the division of power and fought one another. They agreed on one thing only, which was setting restrictions on women's freedoms.

Although women could go to schools and universities and work outside of the home, they had to wear the *hijab* (veil). In addition, the curriculum of schools and universities were all transformed and religious subjects increased to 4-5 subjects in every grade and academic semester. The constitution was also changed to Shariya law, and the Islamic State of Afghanistan was established (Moghadam, 2002). Peace never came with the Mujahideen's arrival to power. The parties started a civil war based on linguistic, ethnic, religious sect and ideological considerations. The war reduced Kabul city to "rubble" and paved the way for the ephemeral Taliban (Dupree, 2002, p. 323).

In September of 1996, an apposition army of religious students, called the Taliban, captured Kabul after bloody skirmishes with the Mujahideen. The Taliban were predominantly Pashtun men who sought only conservative Wahhabi and Deobandi religious training in Pakistani camps in the 1980s, (Dupree, 2002; Rashid, 2000). To Dupree (2002), their "avowed purpose was to cleanse society of the evils" and install a pure Islamic state (Dupree 2002; Rashid, 2000). It was a regime that was only recognized by Saudi Arabia and Pakistan and had no conception of modern governance, democratic or participatory rule, human rights, or women's rights (Dupree, 2002; Moghadam, 2002; and Rashid, 2000).

The Taliban vowed to assuage the civil war and corruption that the Mujahideen had brought to Kabul, but their fanatical gender regime expelled all women from schools and universities and worsened the country's situation. Women became unable to work outside of home. The only job a woman could have was as a doctor or nurse in segregated hospitals and clinics where they could only treat women. This made healthcare very hard for women because there were not enough female doctors (Miller, 2006; Moghadam, 2002). Later, the Taliban outlawed women from shopping or just coming out of their houses without a *mahram*.[16] They also forced women to wear the *burqa* that covered them

---

16   Male kinfolk or her husband.

from head to toe. There were reports that some Taliban raped and married women by force (Miller, 2006; Moghadam, 2002).

Men had other restrictions in the Taliban's decree. They could not shave or style their beards and hair. The Taliban used attendance sheets and forced men to be on time five times a day at mosque for prayer. They prohibited listening to music. They broke peoples' televisions, tape recorders, dish antennas, and audio and video cassettes. They even banned flying kites, a common hobby for Afghans. They even outlawed photography, and owning a camera was a crime. Most of women's public baths were closed down. People were ordered to screen windows in their houses or paint the transparent glass windows so that women could not be seen inside the homes (Rashid, 2000; Moghadam, 2002).

Men and women who would not conform or those who would question their laws and regulations were imprisoned, publicly beaten, tortured, and even executed (Rashid, 2000; Moghadam, 2002). This was even harder and appeared completely alien to Kabuli women (Dupree, 2002, p. 324). The psychological effect of people's fear from the Taliban was devastating. The streets of Kabul were filled with female beggars. War did not end from Kabul and the surrounding areas. The Mujahideen, once enemies, united and started their war against the Taliban dilation. One of the Mujahideen political parties, *Hezb-e-Islami*, led by Gulbuddin Hekmatyar, however, joined the Taliban since their birth. The Mujahideen formed the Northern Alliance. Ahmad Shah Masoud, the leader of Northern Alliance fought the Taliban audaciously until the last moments of his life and never surrendered. Ahmad Shah Masoud was assassinated by two suicide bombers in his office. He is considered the "National Hero" of Afghanistan by some people; however, he is also thought of as a warlord and war criminal by many.

The assassination of Ahmad Shah Masoud happened on September 09, 2001, just two days before the tragedy of September 11, 2001. President George W. Bush declared war against al-Qaida and the Taliban in Afghanistan. The impermanent regime of the Taliban fell apart in less than a week. The United States, along with the Northern Alliance, swept the Taliban out of Kabul. In the Bonn Conference, Hamid Karzai was nominated as the President of the Interim Government of Afghanistan under the supervision of the United Nations. In 2002, Afghanistan had a Transitional Government under Hamid Karzai. Later, Karzai was officially elected by popular vote in 2004 as President of Afghanistan for five more years.

Kabul was in turmoil after the Taliban were out of the capital Both the Afghan government and the international community started rebuilding Afghanistan. At this moment, the Ministry of Women's Affairs was established in 2001 by the Afghan Transitional Administration whose main goal was to ensure the support of Afghan women's social, political, legal, economic, and civic rights. In addition, the Ministry's main purpose was to promote, respect, and fulfill Afghan women's right so that women would be free from all forms of violence and discrimination.

In spring of 2002, schools and universities were reopened for women. According to Afghanistan's Ministry of Education website, by March of 2009 there were about 6.5 million students going to school, and 42% of them were females. The number of women teachers has been also increasing. In addition, Afghan girls once again can travel abroad for education without the government preventing them. Today Afghan women are working both at government and non-government organizations.

About 68 seats are taken by women in the Afghan parliament which is about a quarter of the total seats. This number of female politicians in Afghanistan has been unique in history. In no other previous regimes, have women had this much socio-political influence. Despite all the improvements, however, the country is in a political dilemma and certain issues threaten principles of human rights such as drugs, poverty, corruption, unemployment, illiteracy, and insurgency of the Taliban.

In the current constitution of Afghanistan, no laws can be contrary to the Islamic values (Article 3). Also, article seven of the constitution declares that "the state shall abide by the UN charter, international treaties, international conventions that Afghanistan has signed, and the Universal Declaration of Human Rights" (Constitution of 2004, Article 7). Thus, some contradictions appear between the International Declaration of Human Rights principals and the religion of Islam. Here, freedom of speech, the right to divorce, legal age of marriage, bride-price, segregation of sexes, the polygamous structure of families, and even academic curriculum of schools and universities are dominated and controlled by religious authorities in the Afghan government.

Today people are not allowed to question religion or talk about rights of women outside the boundaries of religion. Divorce is also decided under religious provisions and certain circumstances where women are often vulnerable. Child marriage is still taking place. The bride-price under various names still occurs both religiously and traditionally. Segregation is strictly enforced and women are prevented from taking certain jobs (Dupree, 2002; Rebecca, 2003). The curriculum of schools and universities is not secular either. The system is partially co-educational. In high schools, sexes are segregated. School and university students are required to take Islamic courses every year. In addition, polygamous families with two and occasionally three wives are still prevalent in Afghan society, particularly in rural areas.

Dupree (2002) believes that Afghan society is changing rapidly. She believes gender roles are also changing. According to her, desperate economic needs compel women to work and some husbands do not object. The number of women as family income-earners is increasing. This has changed the social structure of the Afghan family and to Dupree "old prejudices give way to new priorities . . . women need not be so passive, and men must seek new identities" (Dupree, 2002, p. 318).

In short, looking back into the history since Amanullah Khan from 1919 to the present regime under President Hamid Karzai, women have been the center of attention through all system changes in Afghanistan. Monarchy and later regimes none of which were based on the people's will and vote, drafted their own laws and constitutions the way they wanted. Even under the current so called democratic regime under President Hamid Karzai, religion and traditionalism have been interfering with women's basic freedoms, marriage, education, employment, and other issues. Thus, there is an ongoing war between the modernists and traditionalists in Afghanistan for years. Millions fled Afghanistan as a consequence of war and regime changes. The rich and the members of the royal family mostly moved to Europe, Canada, and the United States. Those of the poor remained in Afghanistan or moved to Iran and Pakistan where the number of refugees reached millions.

Marriage Traditions Among Afghan Immigrants in California

In the Afghan culture, marriage is very much structured by religion and traditions (Aseel, 2003; Dupree, 2002; Wahab, 2005). Men, along with pressure from their families, tend to marry Afghan women, preferably their first and usually second cousins. Men also look for women from their own tribe or ethnic group based on religious and linguistic background. The way people get married, the monetary gift that they pay to the bride or the bride family, and marriage to one's cousin, are all predominantly religious traditions. In addition, in the institution of family and marriage, language, religious background, ethnicity, and tribal affiliation of marriage partners play an important role in the Afghan traditional society (Sadat, 2008; Wahab, 2005; Barrenburg, 2003).

In the commonly practiced consanguineous marriage, the couples are predominantly first and second cousins. Studies show that Afghan immigrant families traditionally encourage and even force their sons and daughters to marry their first and second cousins (Wahab 2005; Barrenburg 2003). Caste endogamy, inter-caste marriages, and interactions between tribes play a significant role in the traditional and tribal society in Afghanistan (Wahab, 2005; Barrenburg, 2003).

Ethnic and tribal affiliation plays an important role in Afghan marriages among Afghan immigrants in the United States (Barrenburg, 2003; Dupree, 2002; Lipson and Omidian, 1996; Wahab, 2005). First, families seek to arrange the marriage of their sons and daughters to their cousins. If they could not find a cousin for some reason, the second choice is a bride from their own ethnic group. There are several ethnic groups in Afghanistan with different languages, and religious sects. There have been tensions between the tribes throughout history and that is why most marriages happen between couples from the same tribe, language, and religious sect.

The traditions of dowry, consanguineous marriages, and marriages based on linguistic, tribal and religious affiliations also exist among some Afghan immigrants in the United States. Families constantly try to find girls for their sons from their own relatives. They travel to Afghanistan and sometimes even to Iran and Pakistan for an Afghan girl for their son. Some find a girl from their own ethnic group or sometimes from Afghanistan regardless of the girl's tribe. It rarely happens that an Afghan man seeks a non-Muslim woman who is not from Afghanistan. This could mostly be because of cultural issues and family pressure. Because of the traditional and patriarchal society, the Afghan girl, on the other hand, might find it impossible to marry a non-Afghan man (Barrenburg, 2003; Lipson and Omidian, 1996; Wahab, 2005).

Many Afghan women immigrate to the United States through marriage to Afghan immigrant men. Usually the man's family or siblings go to Afghanistan, meet the girl's family, and bring the bride to America for their son. Rarely, an Afghan man goes to Afghanistan alone to meet the girl and marry her without the help of his family. Accordingly, some Afghan immigrants in the U.S. go to Afghanistan and pick a young beautiful girl for their sons or siblings by paying a bride-price to the girl's family (Aseel 2003, p. 42). Thus, families, particularly the poor and the working class, may not say "yes" on the first day according to the Afghan culture, but later they offer their daughters happily when an Afghan man proposes to their daughter from America or other developed countries. They hope that one day their daughter will send money and support her family back in Afghanistan (Aseel, 2003). The daughter might be happy and expect to find a better life and more freedom when she lives with her husband, although this might not always be the case.

In case of the Afghan immigrant women, Sadat (2008) believes that the older Afghan generation has found it hard to adjust to the American society. Dupree, too, believes that some Afghan immigrant women have become overly dependent because they "could not, or would not, adapt to new surroundings, even refusing to learn English or how to get around by themselves" (Sadat, 2008, p. 319). On the other hand, Lipson and Omidian (1996) and Sadat (2008) believe that most Afghan immigrant men work while they expect their wives to stay home, cook, clean and take care of the children. In their study, some male participants asserted that Afghan women in California prefer to stay home, cook for the family, take care of the children, clean the house, and socialize with Afghan female friends, especially by telephone. In contrast, some Afghan women in Lipson and Omidian's study (1996) claimed that Afghan immigrant women adapted well to the American society. They added that Afghan women drive, work, and speak English and they are more active than their male partners (Lipson and Omidian, 1996; Sadat, 2008).

Some researchers found that family conflict occurs when some Afghan immigrant men in the United States are unemployed while their wives are working (Dupree, 2002; Lipson and Omidian; 1996; Wahab, 2005).When men see their wives as providers of food and shelter for the family they feel intimidated and suffer from a cultural identity crisis about their role as head of the household. Nancy Dupree further states about the Afghan immigrants:

> Few middle-aged and older men, however, were able to pursue the careers in which they had once excelled. This eroded their patriarchal status and left them feeling diminished. Many women, on the other hand, proved to be more flexible in learning to cope. They learned new skills, were willing to take unskilled jobs and thus became the primary breadwinners in many homes, adding further to male sensitivities about their patriarchal prerogatives. (Dupree, 2002, p. 319)

Culturally, Afghanistan is a country where women are traditionally employed as teachers, nurses or doctors. Women hardly ever work at stores, construction, engineering, or other jobs mainly physical work. According to Dupree (2002) woman do every kind of job in the United States to earn a living for their families. Nevertheless, in the United States, although the wife works full-time, the husband still demands that the wife do the house chores, and take care of the children (Lipson and Omidian, 1996; Wahab, 2005).

Fluency in the English language is essential in the United States. Some Afghan women already speak English when they come to America, but those who cannot speak at all confront more hardship. Women who do not speak English may confine themselves at home and may not be able to visit family and friends due to transportation and fear of getting lost. These women are not able to enjoy the regular visiting of family and friends that is a common tradition among Afghans (Lipson and Omidian, 1996). Lack of language skills may disqualify some of the Afghan women who were educated in Afghanistan from securing employment in a job related to their education. American higher educational institutions demand a good command of English and some of these women who do not speak English well might find it more difficult to continue their education. Thus, their choices are limited to staying home.

The control of married and single women is typical among traditional and less egalitarian cultures. Aseel (2003), Dupree (2002) and Lispson and Omidian's (1996) studies also show that the Afghan immigrant single and divorced women are facing social pressures outside of family. Single women "struggle with the mainstream society and their stereotypes about Muslims as fundamentalists and extremists" (Aseel, 2003, p. 43). These women live with their parents and siblings regardless of their age. The father and brothers too try to control their teenage and adult girls about their interaction with other people outside of home.

However, according to Dupree (2002), parents find it hard to convince their sons and daughters about Afghan family and marriage traditions. Sons usually make their own decisions about finding their own partners. They no longer agree to marry their cousins, even second or third cousins. Daughters, too, make their own decisions where to work, who to interact with, and who to marry. Thus, we could conclude that the younger Afghan immigrant generation, particularly those who were born in the United States, or those who were children when they immigrated to United States, have become more independent and do not conform to patriarchal and traditional roles common in Afghanistan.

In addition, the percentage of divorce is much higher among Afghan immigrants in the United States than those in Afghanistan. We could infer from the previous studies that religion and traditions are not affecting the younger Afghan immigrant generation as much as they do in Afghanistan. Here, a woman can get divorced without any fear of violence from the government, traditions, and even her own family. Nevertheless, some studies show that when an Afghan immigrant woman gets divorced, she not only loses her identity as a good woman but also the love of her family (Aseel 2003, Lipson and Omidian 1996; Wahab, 2005). Her family shuns her just because she is divorced. Other families might not propose to her for their son either. These confrontations and social pressures may make her unable or disqualified from marrying again (Lipson and Omidian, 1996; Wahab, 2005). Hence, religious traditions in the Afghan social life have major effects on marriages but the younger generations have adapted to a new social life in Diaspora and pay less attention to traditions and religion largely respected in Afghanistan.

In short, although little has been written about Afghan immigrants in the United States, the existing literature divulges a lot about them. The younger generation, mainly those born in the United States, has been facing identity crises. They consider themselves as Americans but there seems to be a big generational gap between parents and their American-born children. The older generations have kept their Afghan culture and tradition since immigration. Most of these immigrants have been in the United States since the era of the Communists, the Mujahideen, and the Taliban regimes from 1970s to late 1990s. They have been trying to practice the traditions they inherited in Afghanistan. The institution of marriage in particular is majorly influenced by these traditions. The older generations still try to convince their children to marry Afghans who are from their tribe, ethnicity, religious sect, and even second and third cousins, particularly their daughters. Nevertheless, laws in the United States prohibit consanguineous and polygamous marriages in the United States and traditions of bride-price, dowry, arranged marriages, endogamous, and consanguineous marriage practices, highly valued by some parents, no longer make sense to most American-born sons and daughters.

Chapter 3

Methodology

The focus of this study is Afghan immigrant women in California. The goal is to explore the rationalizations of these women who have immigrated to the United States through marriage. The practice of Afghan middle-aged men who go to Afghanistan from the United States and marry much younger women and bring them to America is not openly discussed. People do not always talk about this practice deliberately and neither might they understand it. In order to understand the experiences of the Afghan women in the United States, the narratives and life stories of these women should be heard in their own voices.

The study interviewed eight Afghan immigrant women to determine the extent to which their stories focus on their suffering or their freedom and economical stability in the United States. In addition, the researcher tried to investigate whether these women have been able to seek ways to reverse the traditional script of patriarchy, and whether their marriage to Afghan men in the United States worked for them. To further analyze and interpret data, application of the feminist theoretical perspective was necessary along with the qualitative face to face in-depth interviews with the participants.

THE RESEARCH DESIGN

The current research utilized qualitative research and case study methods based on a feminist epistemological standpoint. The feminist voice-centered method of analysis is used in order to focus on the interviews about the women's concerns and marriage to middle-aged Afghan immigrant men in the United States. With this epistemological standpoint, the focus is on gender inequality in marriage practice, how they draw attention to the oppression and domination of women in society, and how gender inequality is constructed. This method is centrally concerned with hearing the voices of those silenced, othered, and marginalized by the dominant social order (Babbie, 2006). It focuses on the position that women occupy within a social context characterized by a patriarchal sex-gender system (Hesse-Biber, 2005).

The integration of qualitative research and case study methods supported by a feminist epistemological point of view was most appropriate for this research. Through this method, the researcher was able to further analyze the data by attaching meaning and sociological significance to it and by explaining the patterns, categories, and relationships that emerged from the interviews. Therefore, this approach helped to evaluate the underlying meanings of the type of marriages practiced by Afghan immigrants and the narratives of Afghan immigrant women in their own words.

The main objectives of this study were as follows:

1. Explore and describe the subjective experience of Afghan women who immigrate to the United States through marriage.
2. Provide a lucid vision of some facts about marriage traditions that exist among Afghans in general and in particular among women who immigrate to the United States through marriage.
3. Identify the dilemmas that Afghan immigrant women were facing in the United States and in their marriage to Afghan American men.

4. Provide themes about whether they perceived subjugation or freedom.
5. Find out whether they have been able to become independent and find economically stable lives.
6. Contribute to the increasing body of knowledge and literature about the mail-order bride industry, Afghan traditions, and Afghan immigrant women.

Qualitative research through in-depth interviews and case study approach gave a firsthand understanding about the narratives of the Afghan immigrant women in their own words. This method allowed the researcher to explore the meanings of these women's narratives beyond their conversations and responses.

PARTICIPANTS

A non-probability purposive and convenience sample through snowball sampling methods was applied to recruit participants and in order to provide information pertinent to the purpose of this study. The criteria for the participants included age of 18 years or older women. In addition, the requirement was that each woman had come to the United States through marriage to an Afghan immigrant man. The sample in the study included eight married women.

TABLE 1

Participants and their characteristics

Participants (Not real names)	Age	Year of immigration to the U.S.A	Immigration status	Education	Occupation
Frishta	29	2001	Green Card	Grade 8	Unemployed
Nadia	33	1996	Citizen	Bachelor's	Employed
Zohal	34	2005	Green Card	High School	Employed
Farida	37	1991	Citizen	Associate	Employed
Sarah	28	1999	Green Card	Associate	Employed
Maria	30	2000	Green Card	High School	Unemployed
Nahid	29	2004	Green Card	Bachelor's	Employed
Laila	26	2006	Green Card	Bachelor's	Employed

As you can see in Table 1, the age range of the participants was between 26 years old and 37 years old. All participants had lived in the state of California between four and 18 years. Nadia and Farida, who had lived in the United States for 13 and 18 years, had gotten their American citizenship already, whereas other participants, who spent three to 11 years, had green cards only and were not citizens yet. In terms of education, one of the participants, Frishta, was a high school dropout. Two other participants, Zohal and Maria, had high school diplomas only. The five other participants, Nadia, Sarah, Zahra, Laila, and Farida had higher education. These five participants had their associate degrees, bachelor degrees and some wanted to join their master's programs at various higher educational institutions in the United States. Finally, Frishta and Maria were unemployed and the rest of the participants were working either part time or full time.

The researcher already knew three participants, Nadia, Sarah, and Frishta. Through these three participants and the snowball sampling technique, other participants with the same circumstances were found, contacted, and interviewed. In addition, talking to friends and family members helped greatly in finding the participants from California based on the criteria of the sample.

DATA COLLECTION

The data collection for this type of research was based on individual, informal, semi-structured, and digitally recorded in-depth interviewing. Before the interviews, the interview questions (Appendix A), the consent form (Appendix B), and the IRB form were approved by the Institutional Review Board at California State University, Fullerton. The consent form was attached along with the interview questions and was given to the participants before the interview started. The participants signed the consent forms and the interview began. They answered some demographic and as well as semi-structured and open-ended questions. The questions were only about themselves and relating to the research questions. The questions that were ask of interviewing the participants were as follows:

INTERVIEW QUESTIONS

All the interviews were conducted in Persian (Farsi-Dari). The participants answered open-ended questions. The questions were simply worded, and included the following:

DEMOGRAPHIC QUESTIONS

1. How old are you?
2. Education level?
3. Occupation?

INTERVIEW QUESTIONS

1. Tell me about your family? (Father, mother, brothers, sisters and their occupations, and where they live)
2. Tell me about your family in the US? (Husband, children and others in the family and their occupations?)
3. How did you meet your husband?
4. Describe your wedding? (Where and how you got married? Was there any monetary issue involved?)
5. Tell me about how you are experiencing life in the United States?
6. What are the things you like most about your experience in the United States?
7. What are the things you do not like about your experience in the United States?
8. What major challenges do you face in America (In the family and at work)?
9. What was your perception of the United States while in Afghanistan before moving to the United States? And what did you find that differed from your expectation?
10. How did you perceive American women before you immigrated to the US?

11. How many times have you been married? Is your current husband your first spouse?
12. Did you ask your father or mother about your husband/ somebody you wanted to marry?
13. Were you in contact with somebody/your husband before you married him?
14. Did you ask your husband in the US to call your parents and ask them about marrying you?
15. How do you compare yourself to Afghan women in Afghanistan and American women here in California?

All participants were interviewed individually. The interviews were carried out by the researcher, a 24-year-old male Afghan graduate student at California State University, Fullerton. The interviews were scheduled at the convenience of the participants. Each interview was conducted in one session informally, either at the participant's residence, campus library, or somewhere convenient such as a coffee shop or café. The interviews varied in length, from 75-105 minutes. All the interviews were digitally recorded with the consent of the participants.

The researcher was also the interviewer. He engaged in conversation with the participants and gave each of them a verbal introduction in order to set up the interview. He encouraged the participants to answer the questions and to freely describe their life experiences. In order to prevent any type of misunderstanding, the questions were rearticulated and rephrased when necessary during the interviews. In addition, the participants could skip or decline responding to any question that they did not feel comfortable answering. Also, the interviewer was careful not to incorporate his opinions but to allow the participant to take the lead and speak freely about her narratives. The participants were allowed to do most of the talking.

At the end of the interviews, the respondents were thanked for taking part in the interviews and sharing their life stories frankly. After the interviews were conducted, the researcher gave them the opportunity to ask further questions if any. They were each reassured of the confidentiality of their interviews.

There was no risk for the participants. There was no compensation for them either. Prior to the face to face interviews, the informed consent forms were distributed to all participants in their native Afghan language of Persian (Farsi-Dari) in which all participants were fluent. The informed consent form was attached in both English and Persian languages to the questionnaires. All interviews are confidential. No names, addresses, or any kind of identification appear in the study. The data is collected from participants to the extent allowed by the law in the United States.

The digital data was kept in a locked desk until the interviews were transcribed in a word processing file on a computer. The participants were interviewed between July 28 and August 29, 2009. The interview data were transcribed soon after the interviews were conducted. The audio files were deleted permanently on August 30, 2009.

Although the participants did not get any monetary or material benefits, the researcher promised to give each of them a summary of the research findings or a copy of the thesis once completely done. More importantly, the participants confessed that after the interviews, they thought about their lives and marriages in a different way. They also appreciated that the interviews brought many issues to their attention such as their roles in the family, why and how they immigrated to the U.S., and so forth. Some of the participants reassured the researcher that the responses would be completely overt and candid.

The participants were also reassured that their participation was very essential and made the research a major contribution to the body of literature concerning mail-order brides and Afghan immigrant women in the United States. At the end of the interviews, all the participants were debriefed. They were notified that the research would be only for exploratory and academic purposes. They were assured that the study was not conducted for any type of business purposes.

DATA ANALYSIS

The taped interviews were listened to and then transcribed into a word processing program on a computer. The transcription was also done in Persian. Each interview transcription was done carefully and word by word, including the interviewer's comments. The comments basically included observation of respondent's feelings, actions, emotions and so forth. The eight interviews were transcribed in 108 pages, which was a thorough description of the respondents' narratives.

The researcher began reading and thinking about the interview transcriptions. While highlighting major points, the field notes including the respondents' emotions and looks during the interview were also added. The participants' sounds and tone of voices, feelings, and looks were important factors for further understanding and interpreting their voices. The researcher looked for quotes that fit together, quotes that were the most telling, as well as quotes that were problematic.

In the coding process, first the researcher looked for major concepts and themes within the transcribed interviews with the eight participants. Then, the concepts were clarified by categorizing the codes into more focused and analytical codes that included themes, patterns, and descriptive units related to research questions. While grouping the focused concepts and their relationships to one another, they were also analyzed and interpreted simultaneously. The focused themes were translated into English. Finally, by application of a feminist theoretical standpoint and Charlotte Perkins Gilman's theory, the themes were interpreted and analyzed further.

CHALLENGES AND FRUSTRATION OF DATA COLLECTION

The major challenge the researcher would face during the research would be the researcher's identity as an Afghan male interviewing Afghan women. It was feared that the Afghan immigrant women might not agree to participate in the interview and tell their stories to the researcher who was yet another Afghan man.

The researcher thought the participants might be curious and ask questions regarding the research, personality, motivations, and why the researcher wanted to conduct this research. Knowing the purpose of the research and that the researcher was a sociology graduate student, the participants felt comfortable to speak about their life experiences in the United States.

Approaching the other participants through friends and the three already available participants, made it easier and more comfortable for respondents to take part and share their narratives. Nevertheless, the major challenge was to convince the women to participate. Finding these women was not easy. Many refused to participate in the research with different excuses. Most refusals were without any reason. Since it was a snowball method, the participants who already participated requested other women they knew in order to participate as well. Unfortunately, many refused to participate. The reasons were even more disappointing.

One of the major reasons was the husband not permitting the wife to participate. Some women simply said "sorry" and that their husbands would not permit them to be interviewed. The second major reason for three women's refusal to participate in the interview occurred when they read the informed consent form and questionnaire and then changed their mind to participate. Probably it was the content of the consent form and concepts such as "law," "confidential," "digital recording," and other personal questions regarding their personal lives that the women were not willing to participate. One woman refused to continue after answering the third question in the survey.

Chapter 4

RESULTS AND FINDINGS

The goal of the results and findings section is to explore the responses to the interview questions with Afghan immigrant women. The results are basically the summary of what each participant discusses. Each participant has a story to tell. They discuss both subjugation and freedom. Some have either found or they are in the process of seeking opportunities that help them in order to become economically self-sufficient and independent. However, some others have neither adapted well to the American society nor see any change in their lives.

The women were not very talkative when asked the questions. Most of them tended to answer the questions shortly. Some did not talk much but were willing to answer all questions and freely discuss their stories. The researcher tried to rephrase the questions and ask additional related questions in different words in order to encourage the participants to freely describe their circumstances.

In short, the answers focus upon narratives in which these women face dilemmas in their marriage relationships. Also, the focus is on stories in which the women have been able to find subversive ways to challenge patriarchal norms as well as become economically independent. Therefore, the major goal of this section is to find out whether marriage to the Afghan American men have worked for these women and brought good luck, freedom, financial stability, and a happy life, or whether it has caused domination and subjugation.

Each Participant's Narrative

The following is the summary of stories from eight Afghan immigrant women who participated in the study. These women introduce major conceptions of what it means to marry an Afghan American man and immigrate to the United States. Nevertheless, some of the participants talk about their husbands' way of thinking and behavior about the marriage, which is not part of the scope of this research. Their husbands have to be interviewed separately and what they think about their marriage to women from Afghanistan. Therefore, the focus is on what the Afghan women think, not what their husbands think about them and the marriage. The names used in this research are aliases and do not represent the real identity of the participants. The following narratives are basically the summary of answers from the interviews.

The 29-Year-Old Frishta

The interview with Frishta was one of the most interesting interviews. Her life story was full of hopes, dilemmas, and bitter experiences as well. Frishta was very interested in participating in the study and she was very hospitable. She invited the interviewer for lunch and let him interview her in her apartment. Her apartment was nice and tidy. She had old photos of Kabul all over the walls in her living room. She had been married since 2001 to an Afghan American man in California.

Frishta was born in Kabul. She has two brothers and three sisters. Two of her sisters are studying at Kabul Education University, and one is still in high school. Her brothers are in high school. Her father is a shopkeeper in Kabul and her mom is a housewife. Frishta's family never migrated out of Afghanistan, even during the civil war and the Taliban regimes.

Frishta remained uneducated and her family was displaced from their house twice because of the civil war during 1990s in Kabul. Her family moved to safer neighborhoods inside of Kabul city because the severe civil war erupted in 1993. She was in the 8th grade when the Taliban came to power in Kabul in 1996. Frishta was deprived of going to school because the Taliban closed all educational institutions for girls and women. She continued to read story books and study at home during the Taliban but she could no longer continue her formal education. In 2001 she got married.

When asked how she met her husband, Frishta said she had seen her husband about 20 years ago when she was a child when they lived in Afghanistan. Her husband is her father's cousin. Frishta saw her husband at the day of the engagement after almost two decades. Frishta's husband had immigrated to the United States during the communist era in Afghanistan.

In 2000, Frishta's husband visited Kabul with his mom and sister. They proposed to Frishta and promised to take her to the United States. Frishta's family was glad that they had a *khastgar* for her from the United States. Her *gala* was 10,000 dollars. The engagement, *shab-e-khina*[17] (henna night), and the wedding parties were held at a wedding hall in Kabul. About 100 people were invited to her engagement party and about 450 to the wedding party. Approximately a total of $15,000 was spent for their marriage. It took about three months until Frishta got her visa and came to the United States.

Currently, Frishta lives in California. She has two daughters. One of her daughters is three years old and the other is five. Frishta's husband is 12 years older than her. He has two jobs. He works full time at an insurance company. In addition, he works at a restaurant in the evenings. Frishta's husband works 50-60 hours a week. They have many relatives in California. Almost all of them are her husband's immediate family members and relatives.

---

17   *Shab-e-khina* is one night before the wedding party and includes as much ritual as the wedding night. Traditionally, in this night the groom and bride exchange rings, adorn each other's hands with henna, and there is music and dance among close relatives including cousins, aunts and uncles. During the *shab-e-khina* usually there are not a lot of men present.

When Frishta first came to the United States, she liked it a lot. She said all the facilities such as water, washing and drying machines, gas, 24-hour electricity, cleanliness, and so forth were all privileges she did not have in Kabul. She added:

> Peace is good in America. There is no war here. In Afghanistan we were always afraid. I could not go outside of home. Every day I was worried that my family would be tortured, beaten, and even killed by the Mujahideen or the Taliban. Here in the US, I never worry about those things. My husband has a job and we don't have financial problems. I like the weather here. I like the people in America. I like everything.

Most of the focus on Frishta's experience of life in Afghanistan was a portrait of fear, war, and threat. She thought most women in Afghanistan do not and cannot provide good nutrition for themselves and for their children. She also thought in Afghanistan there are no jobs for people and there is poverty by which women, particularly widows and also orphans, are affected the most. Nevertheless, Frishta thought, life in America is not like that and people do not suffer from hunger, war, and fear. Frishta, however, missed her family and relatives in Afghanistan a lot.

Frishta was 27 years old at the time of the current study. She is the only member from her family in the United States. She does not have anybody from her family or close relatives in the United States. She misses her family a lot and has only gone to Afghanistan to visit them twice in the last nine years. She visited her family in 2005 and last year in 2008 as well. Frishta calls her family at least twice a month. She sends them 200 to 300 dollars every month. She wants her family to move closer to her but she thinks it is very hard to get them to the United States. She believes it is better for her family to move to the United States because of security reasons and as well as better educational and other opportunities.

Frishta thought of herself as the same as other women in Afghanistan. However, she thinks she is luckier than them because she has a more convenient life than some of those back in Afghanistan. In regards to comparing herself to American women, she thought she was the same as some who were family oriented and who stayed home. However, she believed that it was not good that some women do not stay home and they are working outside of the home and leave their children for babysitters. She thought it is necessary for a woman to stay home and take care of the children.

Frishta does not face any major challenges in America. The only thing that bothers her is loneliness and being away from her family. She also thinks she has not adapted well to the American society because of the lack of English language skills and transportation problems. She got her driver's license two years ago but she does not want to drive much. She only drives for shopping or taking her children to the nearby park. She hoped to get her family to the United States as soon as she gets her citizenship. She has applied for their visa but they will not be able to come to the United States until she gets her citizenship. She hopes to get her citizenship next year.

When asked why it took so long for her to get her citizenship, Frishta said the reason was the requirement of a good command of the English language in order to pass the test. She also mentioned that visiting Afghanistan twice in the last few years delayed her citizenship. She was anxious about the citizenship and wanted to become a citizen as soon as possible because then she can sponsor her family.

THE 33-YEAR-OLD NADIA

Nadia was born in the city of Kandahar in Afghanistan. Her father was a farmer and her mother was a religious teacher in her village in Kandahar. Now both Nadia's parents live with her in the United States. Neither of them works because they do not speak English now. Nadia has one brother who is in college and still lives in Kandahar.

Nadia was a teenager when the civil war broke out. Her family was displaced from their house during the civil war and the Taliban regimes. She did not stop going to school. She graduated from high school in 1994 before the Taliban entered Kandahar city. The hope for continuing her education did not exist any longer when the Taliban infested the city. Her brother quit school when he was in 10th grade. The economy worsened for Nadia's family so much that her brother could not afford to commute to school. Nadia's family decided to move to Quetta in mid 1995. Her father worked in a bakery in Quetta and supported his entire family by himself. In 1996 Nadia got married.

Nadia got married to her cousin's brother-in-law, Ramin, who had lived in the United States since the 1980s during the Communist regime. Ramin was 16 years older than her. Nadia had never met Ramin before. She actually saw her husband on the engagement day. Nadia's cousin, Jamila had immigrated to the United States in 1993. Jamila recommended Nadia to Ramin's family in California while Nadia was in Quetta.

Nadia said that Ramin's mother had gone to Quetta alone in order to propose to her for her son. The next month Ramin was in Quetta for the engagement party. Nadia left Quetta with her husband three and a half months after their engagement and *nikah*. Nadia did not have a wedding party in Quetta because they did not have many relatives that lived there. She had a small invitation of 20-30 people, mostly family, friends, and distant relatives, for both her engagement and wedding parties that were on the same day.

Nadia's family did not mind her not having a big wedding party. They said it would not be very safe to go to Kandahar for the wedding either. Ramin, having offered $12,000 for her *mahr* and *jawab-e-shirini*, married and brought Nadia to America. In California, they had a gathering of more than a hundred people, mostly Ramin's relatives and friends for their marriage celebration.

Nadia has lived in California since 1997. Today she has three children, two boys and a girl. Her daughter is 11 and her two sons are 8 and 9 years old. Ramin is an auto mechanic and he has got his own garage and mechanic shop in California. He is educated and has a bachelor's degree in engineering and teaching credentials. Nadia got her bachelor's degree 2 years ago. She has been a primary school teacher since 2007. Nadia said she has a normal, happy life.

Nadia has always liked the United States. In her opinion the United States is much better than where she lived in Quetta and in Kandahar. She emphasized on peace, security, freedom, and educational opportunities in the United States. She was hopeful about Afghanistan's future. She thought peace has already come to Afghanistan and things are getting better.

Three years ago, the only thing Nadia worried about and missed for years in the United States was her family before they immigrated to the United States. Her brother, however, could not come to the United States because he was above the age of 18 and did not speak English. He got married instead and today he has three children. He works and lives in Kabul. Nadia's parents have been going to Afghanistan every year to visit their relatives and their only son left in Afghanistan.

Nadia thought of herself as a very independent woman. She said she would not have been able to continue her education and become independent if she were still living in Quetta or in Kandahar. She thought of herself as more fortunate than most women in Afghanistan, who do not have access to education and other freedoms. More specifically about freedom (or lack of it), she stressed education. She thought women who have no education are not free because they are not able to contribute to their family and also raise children well. She further stated:

> Afghan women unfortunately do not know who they are. They should go to school. Each father should send his daughter to school. They should become educated mothers like ones here in America. Most women are educated and they are working here in the United States. I think working is freedom and if women do not work they are not free.

Nadia did not face any major challenges in the United States. However, she was worried about losing her job because of the recent economic recession in 2009. Some of the teachers from her school were laid off in the past few months and she was worried about that too. Overall,

Nadia did not have a major complaint about life in the United States. Lack of English language skills was a major challenge for her for the first two years in the United States. Later, she took English as well as citizenship classes at one of the junior colleges in addition to raising three children and doing the house chores. Studying English improved her skills and made life much easier for her. She was then able to get her citizenship in three years. Nadia was thankful to her husband Ramin for supporting her always.

THE 34-YEAR-OLD ZOHAL

The interview with Zohal took place at a Starbucks café. She was very nervous about participating in the interview. Although she read and signed the consent forms, she asked many questions about the study and why it was being conducted. She over emphasized on the issue of confidentiality of her interview. She did not want people to know about her personal life.

Zohal was born in Kabul. She has four sisters and two brothers. Her brothers and two of her sisters are in college. Her two other sisters are working for the Afghan government. Her father is working for the government too but her mom is a teacher at a private school. They are all in Kabul.

Zohal's family migrated to Pakistan during the civil war in 1993 but repatriated back to Afghanistan after four months. Zohal speaks about her experience in Pakistan as follows:

> The weather was unbearably hot in Peshawar. The Pakistani police stopped my dad and brothers on the street all the time and took their money. We could not afford to rent an apartment. The eight of us lived in two rooms on the second floor of a house. We had to pay fees for our education and because none of my parents found a job we could not continue our studies. That is why although the civil war was worsening in Kabul, we went back to Kabul and tried to live in a safer neighborhood. We chose to stay in Kabul for several years

afterwards even though the Taliban closed schools for girls. We did not have any other choice.

Zohal was in Kabul when Javed's parents went to her family for *khastgari* in 2001. Javed was Zohal's distant relative from her mom's family side. Javed also went to Kabul from the United States because of *khastgari*. Javed's entire family was in Kabul and they have never been to the United States. Javed is five years older than Zohal. They got married in late 2001. They invited about 600 guests to their wedding party. She said the *toyana* for her marriage was 300,000 Afghanis which is approximately $6,000 and it was paid to her parents. In total, about 20,000 dollars was spent for her wedding expenses including the *toyana*, jewelry, clothes, dinner for about 600 people, music, and so forth.

Javed had promised to take Zohal to the United States but was unable to do so for four years. He left his wife in her family's home and came to the United States to prepare travel documents and sponsorship for his wife. Months later Zohal had her first baby son while Javed was in the United States. Two years later they had their second child while Javed was in the United States. For four years Javed visited his wife and children once a year until he was able to bring them to the United States in 2005. Zohal said the reason why their immigration to the United States took so long was because of her two children who were born in Kabul.

Zohal works part time at a mall and she raises two children. Zohal's husband Javed works at a restaurant in California. They have two daughters who are both in elementary school. The money they are both making is enough for the rent and other expenses. Javed's uncle's family is in California also. His other relatives are all in Afghanistan. Zohal, on the hand, does not have any family or relatives in the United States.

Zohal's first impression of the United States was the cleanliness and peace in America but she still thinks life in Afghanistan is better. To her life without family and relatives is meaningless. She said:

> Of course when a girl gets married she goes to a new family and meets her in-laws. For me and Javed in California there is only work, eat, and sleep. We have almost no rela-

tives here. It is only Javed's uncle's family who we visit most of the time. It is good they are here. I am happy that we know some Afghan families and our American neighbors. Sometimes we go and visit them but honestly we do not enjoy our *Eid, Nawroz*, or anything. I think life is very short and boring here. Afghanistan was much better. I wish peace comes soon so all Afghans go back to Afghanistan from every corner of the world.

Zohal thought interaction with other relatives and spending time with family is very important. To Zohal, Afghan people have very good and interesting lives, but unfortunately, war and poverty has made many people unfortunate. She also thought Afghans have a good culture of visiting one another often but that is not possible for them in America because families are always busy and do not have the time for much interaction and visiting. Zohal has a car and a full-time job but she still thinks life is not interesting for her. Her major challenge in the United States is boredom because of a lack of interaction and constant visiting of family and relatives as she had in Kabul.

When asked how Zohal compared herself to women in Afghanistan and in America, she said:

Some women in Afghanistan have better lives than I do and some do not. I think there are a lot of poor women and widows in Afghanistan, which is unfortunate. I am not poor. I am working here in California. Some Afghan women also work and are happy, but some do not have an education, any English language or computer skills. Some might have bad husbands who are strict and do not let them go to school or work. So I think I am happier than most but some might be happier than I am.

Zohal thinks it is better for her and her husband to be living and also working in Afghanistan. She speaks English well and thinks adaptation to the American society is not hard. Nevertheless, to her life is short and it has to be spent with family and friends and working for Afghanistan.

THE 37-YEAR-OLD FARIDA

Farida is a 37-year-old woman and she has three children. She has been in the United States since 1991. She lives in San Diego. Her entire immediate family has been in the United States since 1991. Farida is an American citizen. She has a bachelor's degree in business finance and she works at a real estate agency. In addition, she does hair dressing for her own business in the evenings and on the weekends.

Farida was born in Kabul. Her parents live in Northern California. Her father is working at a car dealership and her mom is a kindergarten teacher. Farida has two brothers. Her older brother is a mechanic. He is married and has two children. Her younger brother has studied law and he is married too. Her older brother lives in Northern California but her younger brother lives in San Diego and he is still getting ready for his bar exam. Farida's family came to the United States in 1991.

Farida's family wanted to leave Afghanistan during the first Communist regime under President Taraki but they waited for a better social change in Afghanistan. As years passed, and President Taraki and later President Hafizullah Amin were killed, the situation in Afghanistan became worse. They still waited and lived in Afghanistan until two more presidents came to power, Babrak Karmal and Dr. Najibullah. Farida's family thought things were getting better since the Soviets were leaving Afghanistan. However, they saw that the situation is worsening because of the Mujahideen threatening Dr. Najibullah's so-called Communist puppet government. Thus, Farida's family decided to leave Afghanistan in 1991 before the fall of Dr. Najibullah's government. The same year Farida got married to Behroz, who had immigrated to the United States about six years before her family did.

Behroz is actually Farida's second cousin from her father's relatives. Behroz's family used to live close to Farida's childhood home in Kabul. In Afghanistan, the two families visited each other often. Behroz's family knew the situation in Afghanistan was worsening, and they left Afghanistan earlier. They were still in contact with Farida's family and insisted on their leaving the country also, but Farida's family was hopeful about the situation getting better and therefore, they waited.

Farida was about 19 years old when Behroz's father called her from the United States and proposed her for Behroz. Farida described it as follows:

> Uncle Maher (Behroz's father) called my parents and proposed me to his oldest son, Behroz. It was completely unexpected. My father told him that he agreed with their proposal but wanted my happiness and consent as well. I knew Behroz was a wonderful person and he was educated too. I was happy to marry him; so I did. My decision to marry Behroz also changed our destiny in that my family decided to move to the United States.

A few weeks later, Behroz and his parents came to Afghanistan to visit Farida's family and also as an official *khastgari*. The same week they received *shirini* and offered about $1000 as *jawab-e-shirini* to Farida's family. They prepared a small gathering of relatives for the engagement party in a few days. Two weeks after their engagement, the families decided to celebrate the wedding in Kabul before they left for the United States. Hence, they decided to get married in Farida's house. They invited about 60 people for *shab-e-khina* and 300 people for the wedding. According to Farida approximately $5,000 was spent for jewelry, clothes, gifts, food and so forth.

Today Farida is very happy in the United States. She enjoys her time with her two teenage sons and her 11-year-old daughter, who are all in school. She thinks her family was lucky to move out of Afghanistan before the Mujahideen, and the Taliban regimes in 1990s. She thinks if they were in Afghanistan, they would have gone through poverty or they would remain ignorant and uneducated because there were barely any schools opened during the war. She could imagine how oppressive and despotic the Taliban regime was against Afghan women.

Compared to Afghan women in Afghanistan, Farida thought of herself as luckier than most because she is in the United States. Also she felt lucky because she got married to an educated man and somebody she knew. She loves the United States. She said in Afghanistan life was very hard for people during the Communist regime. Today too, she thinks life is hard because of the Taliban threat to women who go to school or work in Afghanistan. Farida enjoys her job, particularly her own business of hairdressing. She said her customers are increasing all the time.

Farida enjoys life a lot in California. She has many Persian, Indian, Pakistani, and Afghan friends in addition to her American friends. In addition, she said about seven families live in California who are her and Behroz's close relatives. Farida has been to many amusement parks and beaches in California with her family and she loves it. She thinks there is a lot of freedom in America and the rule of law is very good. Farida is not worried about war, poverty, people to deprive her of her freedoms, and so forth. She thought in America everybody is free to do whatever they want to do unless it is illegal. She thought America was definitely a better society with real freedom.

Farida thought there would be no problems in America before she came here. However, today she thinks that problems exist everywhere. Some of her relatives were laid off during the 2009 economic recession. She hoped that her family's jobs are not taken from them too. Other than that she did not have any other challenges in her life experience in the United States.

THE 28-YEAR-OLD SARAH

The interview with Sarah took place at her home. She was one of the other young participants who had some interesting narratives from her life experience both in Afghanistan and later in the United States. She got married to an Afghan man, Ali, and immigrated to the United States in 1999.

Sarah comes from a large family. She has three brothers and four sisters. They are all college educated except for her two younger brothers, who are still in high school. Her father is a college professor at Kabul University and her mother is a housewife. Her family never immigrated out of Afghanistan during the bloody regimes of the Communists, the Mujahideen, and the Taliban. Her family was lucky to have an educated father who was a professor. He taught his children, particularly his daughters, at home when schools were closed for them by the Taliban for more than five years. She remembers the tough days in Afghanistan. That was the worst time in her life when she quit school and lost almost all her school friends.

When asked how Sarah met her husband, she said she knew him through one of her cousins. Ali is a relative of Sarah's cousin's husband. Ali is nine years older than Sarah. He immigrated to the United States in 1989. Sarah's cousin, who lives in Afghanistan, had talked to Ali about Sarah and told him that she had found him a girl. After some time Ali's family first sent Ali's photo and then proposed to Sarah through her cousin, who still lives in Afghanistan. Sarah's family agreed with the proposal from Ali's family. A week later, Ali's mother was in Afghanistan and proposed to Sarah officially.

After approval of *khastgari*, Ali also went to Afghanistan in 1999, got married and came back to the United States. In less than three months Sarah came to the United States as well. Ali gave $6,000 as *shirbaha* and $2,500 as *jawab-e-shiri* to Sarah's parents in addition to the jewelry, reception for about 150 people, wedding dresses, musical band, the decorated limousine and other expenses that cost an additional $8000-$10000. Sarah described her marriage:

> Ali and I remained engaged for one month and then we got married. Our wedding was at a nice hall in Kabul. About 150 guests had been invited for dinner and most of them were my relatives. Almost all of Ali's immediate family and close relatives are in the United States and in Europe. That is why we did not have a very large wedding ceremony. It was an unforgettable memory that on my wedding day, some of my family members and relatives were sad and cried because they knew Ali would be taking me to the United States.

Currently, Sarah has three children. Her sons are five and seven years old, and her daughter is nine. Ali has a bachelor's in computer science and Sarah has an associate degree. She is a receptionist at a company and she likes her job. Sarah's parents-in-law also live in the same apartment with them in California. Sarah likes her parents-in-law and thinks they are very nice to her. In addition, she thinks without their help, raising her three children would be impossible while going to college and work.

Sarah was happy and satisfied with her life in the United States. She said in 1999 when she first came to the United States, she went through culture shock for months. She noticed the differences between the American society and Afghan society where the Taliban were ruling. The first thing that caught her attention was the women in America who had freedom, and who worked and had a normal life as men. She also thought peace, the facilities, and a comfortable life in the United States was everything she desired.

Sarah learned how to speak English a little bit from her father in Kabul. When she came to California, Ali helped her focus on her language skills and education. Three years after her stay in California, Sarah was able to join a community college. After two years, she transferred to a university and has almost finished her bachelor's in biology with a minor in chemistry. Sarah thought the university turned her into a new person, with new goals in her life and for her family.

Sarah thinks of herself as a very fortunate woman who has access to education and technology. Sarah will continue her education. She will start her master's program soon after she has her bachelor's. She thinks education is the key to success. She also has been volunteering with some nongovernmental organizations in southern and northern California that are working for Afghanistan. Sarah appreciated NGOs who are working on women's capacity building and other training skills such as embroidery, tailoring, nursing, teaching, and other skills. She, however, thinks that NGOs and the Afghan government should focus on educating women. She stressed that the government educational institutions should make high school mandatory for both men and women. She also emphasized that families should not be allowed to deprive their daughters and sons of going to schools.

Sarah does not face any major challenges in the United States today. What makes her feel homesick is not seeing her family. She has been visiting them every year but she wishes her family was with her in the

United States. For the first two or three years she missed her family a lot and that was the biggest challenge she had. Today she still thinks if she had her family and more relatives in the United States, life would have been better for her.

Citizenship is the reason that Sarah has not been able to bring her family to the United States in the first few years. Sarah believed school, work, and raising children made it tough for her to get her citizenship sooner. She has her final citizenship interview in 3 months.

THE 30-YEAR-OLD MARIA

Maria's life and her experience in California were filled with challenges and also happiness. Maria was born in the city of Herat in Afghanistan. Currently, her father is a government employee in Afghanistan. Her mom is a housewife. She has two brothers who are both working as translators with international and nongovernmental organizations in Herat.

Maria's family always lived in Herat city. In 1998, her family was forced to leave their house in Herat province because of the Taliban arrival to the city. Maria had just finished 10th grade in high school when the Taliban declared that the schools for women were shut down. Thus, she was left uneducated for years. In 2000 Maria got married to Navid who was an Afghan man living in the United States for a while. The same year she immigrated to the United States.

Maria is Navid's uncle's granddaughter. In 1999 his aunt recommended Maria to him. Navid started to call and e-mail Maria while she was in Afghanistan. Navid told Maria all about his life and ex-wife before he officially proposed to her through his mother. Navid immigrated to Sweden in 1991 and in 1996 he had married a Swedish girl. He also fathered a son from his Swedish wife. After two years they got divorced; Navid got custody of his son and left Sweden for the United States. Today Navid has his teenage son with him in California. Maria thought Navid was an educated man and that her life would also change for the better if she moved to the United States. She also thought Navid was not a stranger and therefore they would have a good life together.

Maria agreed to marry Navid and about four months later Navid was in Herat for the wedding. Navid had officially sent a *khastgar* (his mother) to Maria's family in order to propose to her. Navid gave 200,000 Afghanis (approximately $4000) for the *shirbaha*. Soon, everything was decided. They did not have an engagement party. With the consent of both families the wedding took place in Herat. They invited approximately 300-350 people for the reception in a wedding hall. In addition, he spent approximately $3000 on a musical band, decorated van, transportation for his guests, and gifts for both his wife and some others such as his *Shahbalah*, his cousins, and his family.

Currently, Maria raises both Navid's teenage son and her own two children. She has two sons, who are four and seven years old. Maria was pregnant at the time of the interview. She did not have a job for over a year. She was working at Target but quit after she got too caught up with raising her sons. She thinks her children would forget Farsi language if she does not practice with them. That is why she chose to spend more time with her children and stay home. Navid's teenage son barely speaks Farsi because Maria thinks they were not around him much and neither she nor Navid paid enough attention to how he spoke Farsi.

Navid works for a cell phone company. He is making enough money to pay the house mortgage and other expenses. He is happy about Maria's decision to help the children more with their homework and language skills. Navid's teenage son goes to a Islamic school in Orange County. Maria believed their sons need to understand their religion and be able to recite the holy Quran. Therefore, she believes sending their children to the Islamic school in Orange County and helping them with their lessons is their priority.

Maria's first impression of the United States was very good. When she was in Afghanistan, she believed that in the United States, continuing her family life and training her children based on Islamic trainings would not be possible. Nevertheless, when she was in Orange County, she saw so many Islamic centers and schools that she was amazed. Since then she started to appreciate the United States because she believed everybody was free to practice whatever religion they want to. In addition, she liked the people, facilities, weather, beaches, traffic laws, human rights, peace, and as she said "almost everything" else.

Maria missed her parents and siblings during the first few months but now she has got used to it. She was happy she found many Afghan and American friends in California. She visits them often and particularly on major American and Afghan holidays. Maria does not have a major challenge in the United States. The only thing she is worried about is her children growing up and getting misguided. Although she believed in freedom of religions in the United States and thought her children could be raised Muslims, she thought there were other ways that they could be misguided such as, gangs, drugs, premarital sex, and so forth.

Maria thinks she was privileged to come to the United States. She believes life is very hard in Afghanistan but here in the United States life is very comfortable. She believes Afghan women in most parts of Afghanistan including the capital, Kabul, face a lot of hardship in both winters and summers. There are not enough resources for a decent life such as gas, water, electricity, and heat, she believes. In addition, she thinks joblessness, poverty, the Taliban threat, and harassment toward women are the major problems that Afghan people in general and, in particular, the Afghan women are facing.

THE 29-YEAR-OLD NAHID

Nahid was a very happy woman with one beautiful daughter who was only 3 years old. The interview with Nahid took place in her house. Nahid seemed like a successful woman. Also, seeing her home and lifestyle one could tell that her life was good from an economical standpoint. She came from an educated family. Her father was a university professor and her mom was an official employee of the Ministry of Foreign Affairs of Afghanistan in the 1970ss and 1980s. Today, Nahid's older brother is working with the Ministry of Foreign Affairs of Afghanistan as well.

Nahid's family lived in Kabul until the Islamic regime took over President Dr. Najibullah's government in 1992. Nahid's father was arrested by some Mujahideen and was declared a Communist. Luckily, he saw a friend of his where he was imprisoned for almost a week. His friend was a witness that Nahid's family was innocent and did not have to do anything with the Communists. The day he was freed, they decided that there was no place for them in Afghanistan any longer. They moved to the neighboring country of Tajikistan for the next eight and a half years.

While living in Tajikistan, Nahid's family was supported financially by one of her uncles who lived in Moscow. In Dushanbe, Nahid and her brother were able to learn basic computer skills and as well as English and Russian. Nahid also completed high school in Tajikistan. Her parents, however, went through hard times because they could not have decent jobs. Finally, they decided to leave Tajikistan and go back to Afghanistan in late 2001 when the Taliban regime fell apart in Afghanistan.

In 2002 Nahid's father had his job back at Kabul University, where he taught for years. In the same year, Nahid enrolled at the English Literature Department at Kabul Education University in Kabul. She was in her second semester when she found a *khastgar* from the United States whose name was Jawad.

Jawad is Nahid's distant relative from her father's *qawm* (clan). He had immigrated to the United States in 2000. In Pakistan he had studied computer science for his bachelor's degree. In the United States he was able to enroll in a master's program in computer science. He got his master's degree in 2005. Jawad is 34 years old today, and he is about five years older than Nahid. Nahid and Jawad knew each other since childhood. They had immigrated to Pakistan the same year and lived in the same city as well. Jawad had promised that Nahid could continue her education in the United States. Hearing that, Nahid and her parents agreed to Jawad's *khastgari*.

Nahid and Jawad got engaged in early 2004. Five months later that year they got married. About four months later the same year she immigrated to the United States. Nahid describes the memory of her wedding memory as follows:

Our engagement took place in our house in Kabul. We had invited approximately 300 people. After five months Jawad came again to Kabul and we got married. Our wedding was held in a beautiful hall in Khair Khana, Kabul. I think we invited about 800-900 people. It was a beautiful evening. *Shab-e-khina* was a lot of fun because all my close relatives came to see me. The night after *Shab-e-khina* it was my wedding. My parents cried a lot on my wedding night.[18] I cried with them too. We both knew I would soon leave them and go far away from them.

When asked about expenses and costs, Nahid was not sure exactly how much money was spent. It seemed like a lot of money was spent in their wedding. The invitation of approximately 300 people to the engagement party, about 50-100 in *shab-e-khina*, and about 800-900 people to the wedding, could cost approximately $30,000. Nahid did not like to wear a lot of gold. She only had a ring and a necklace in her wedding that Jawad had brought with him from the United States. She knew she would not be wearing a lot of gold in the United States, particularly the large necklaces, bracelets, and rings that Afghan women wear in Afghanistan.

About $4000 was paid by Jawad to Nahid's family as *jawab-e-shirini*. According to Nahid there was no demand of a monetary gift of any kind by her family. She said the $4000 was a voluntary *jawab-*

---

18   Parents crying on their daughters' wedding nights is common. It has many reasons. The first reason is crying for happiness because their daughter leaves home with prestige and a good name and gets married to somebody. The second reason is because parents become sad. They cry because they lose their daughter. Almost always the woman leaves her parents' home. She might go to a different province. In these participants' cases for example they leave the country where their parents might not be able to see them for years. Likewise, if the girl has a job and she gets married and leaves her family. Then, she might no longer give her money to her family and thus the family loses a portion of the economic contribution. In addition to all this, the house chores, babysitting, and cooking heavily depend on girls at home. When a girl leaves home, the mother bears the left over load of work and responsibilities as well.

e-shirini that men typically pay as much as they want. She said most of the money was spent for getting her marriage certificate, passport, visa, and trip costs to the American Embassy in Pakistan and back to Afghanistan for immigration purposes.

When Nahid came to the United States, after one year she was enrolled in college. She got her bachelor's degree in education from San Diego State University in 2007, and the same year she got her teaching credential. In early 2008, she got a job as a teacher. She has been working as a full-time teacher since then. Nahid worked on campus at her library while she was a student. She believed working on campus helped her a lot with her language skills and as well as working experience in the United States.

Nahid's major challenge was her baby during her studies. She felt lucky as one of her aunts lived in San Diego and she took care of her baby while she was at school and at work. Even today her aunt has been looking after her daughter although the kindergarten at school has been a great help Nahid thought. Other than raising her baby daughter, Nahid thought there were no other challenges in her life. She believed math, writing, and some other subjects were very hard for her for the first two years. She put more time and dedication to her studies and successfully got her bachelor's. She hopes to get her Master's degree once her daughter is old enough to go to school.

Nahid thought she was a very lucky woman that she immigrated to the United States and married an educated man like Jawad. She thought Afghan women have been suffering because of war, poverty, and loss of husbands and children during the thirty years of war. She thought Afghan women who could immigrated to Pakistan or Iran, or Tajikistan during the crises in Afghanistan, were luckier because they could at least continue their education or learn some basic computer and English language skills. However, those who were left in Kabul suffered a lot during the civil war and the Taliban regimes because of their rights and deprivation of going to schools. Nahid is optimistic about Afghan women now and she thinks that by becoming more educated, Afghan women will be able to make their own lives better.

Nahid is not a citizen yet but she hoped to get her citizenship by early 2010. She has been going to Afghanistan to visit her family almost every year. Her parents like to live in Kabul. Her brother, however, wants to come to the United States with his wife and three children.

THE 26-YEAR-OLD LAILA

Laila was the last participant in the study. She was a young 24-year-old smart woman born in the city of Kabul. She was happy to participate in the interview. She has two sisters and one brother. Her sisters are in college in Kabul, but her brother Ajmal is in the United States. He is a recent college graduate and he is working. Laila's father was a government employee of Afghanistan's Ministry of Information and Culture during the Communist regime and also during 2002 and 2003. Now, her father works at the United Nations office as a driver because he has a much better salary. Her mom is a housewife, and she is in Kabul too.

Laila and her family suffered a lot during the Communist regime, the Civil War, and the Taliban regimes. Laila's uncle was abducted during the Hafizullah Amin government and has been missing since then. Her father was imprisoned for four months during Dr. Najibullah's government for no reason. Later during the Civil War, they went through poverty and also threats from various political parties. She describes it as follows:

> My family never liked to participate in political parties because it was dangerous. Regimes kept changing and they did not like one another. Each party asked my father to carry a gun and join the *jihad* which was, in fact, "Afghans fighting against other Afghans." When my father refused to get a weapon and join them, he was imprisoned, interrogated, beaten, and threatened. That made our family flee from one city to the other. We lived in Dehmazang in Kabul, but it was never safe during the Civil War. Finally, the situation worsened and we fled to Iran in 1994.

Laila's family went through hard times while escaping from the Civil War. They faced a lot of trouble passing through the Afghan-Iranian border. They got detained by the Iranian police and were deported. They spent almost a week in some motels on the Afghan-Iranian border but tried to pass the border again. The second time they were successful to arrive in Taftan city and later in Mashhad city, where they had a relative.

In Iran, Laila and her siblings found it hard to go to school. They were somehow able to get enrolled because her father knew a friend who helped in getting his children enrolled in a public high school. They learned English in a private institution, although they could barely afford it. Laila's father worked at a factory and her mom worked in a dairy farm. In 2003, Laila and her siblings were all high school graduates but could not get enrolled at Iranian universities. They were also hopeful about the situation in Afghanistan that the Taliban were out of power and there was peace. They were hopeful to continue their education in Afghanistan. Thus, they decided to move back to Afghanistan in 2003.

Laila got into Kabul University in 2004 and in the same year she got engaged to one of her distant relatives. Three months later her fiancé asked her to leave the university and to not continue her education anymore, for no reason. That is how Laila and her family decided to break the engagement, even though Laila's fiancé was one of their relatives. Laila continued her education at Kabul University until 2006 when she found a *khastgar*, Hamid, from the United States.

Hamid is 34 years old and he has been in the United States for over 15 years. Laila's classmate Maryam was her best friend at Kabul University. Maryam talked to Laila about her brother Hamid, who lived in the United States. She had told Laila that Hamid was educated and that they were a good match for each other. That is how Laila agreed to marry Hamid. In late 2005, Hamid sent his parents from California as *khastgars* to Laila's home in Kabul. The two families agreed on basic issues. They wanted to make sure Hamid was not a drug addict or an uneducated person and that he would not be strict on Laila's education and work freedom.

In two months, Hamid traveled to Afghanistan and got married at a wedding hall in Kabul. They did not have a big engagement party. Also, because Hamid had to return to California for his job, they decided to get married as soon as possible. In about three and a half weeks all the arrangements were made for their wedding. Wedding cards were distributed and about 500 people were invited. One week after the marriage Hamid flew back to California.

Laila came to the United States after four and a half months by herself. She said she had to go to Islamabad and the American Embassy in Kabul for immigration and to get a visa. Her father accompanied her during four visits to the American Embassy in Islamabad. She was finally able to travel to the United States in December of 2006 by herself. She explained her experience:

> I had never been on an airplane before. I got lost in the Dubai airport and missed my flight to New York. I asked for help and I got another flight about seven hours later. From New York, I had to take the flight to California. That was another four-hour wait in the airport. My husband's family and also my family in Kabul were very worried about why I did not call them. In the airport, I asked somebody for his phone to make a call. I was relieved when I was able to call Hamid about two o'clock in the morning. Around 7:30 a.m. I caught a connecting flight to California. In total, I spent about two days en route.

When Laila arrived in California her relatives and in-laws had already come to receive her at the airport in the afternoon. She said she went through culture shock and could not think normally for several days and weeks. She said her new home, husband, in-laws, people, and everything and everywhere around her seemed like a dream to her during the culture shock. Laila has been in the United States since 2006. She has got an eight-month-old baby daughter. Hamid has studied business and he works at an insurance company. Laila has finished junior college. She is planning to continue her education and get her bachelor's in computer science. She has a green card and said she is trying to seek citizenship. She has bought the books and thinks she will be ready earlier next year.

Laila said she has a very happy and comfortable life. She remembers the bad days that her family spent in Iran and in Afghanistan. She thinks Afghanistan may take a very long time to become peaceful because the illiteracy rate is very high and all people know is about war and bloodshed. She was hopeful and happy about the presence of the United States and international community in Afghanistan.

When asked if she has any major challenges in the United States, she mentioned culture shock and her worry about her family's safety in Afghanistan. She said she did miss her family but thought talking to them almost every week helped her homesickness. Also, she was able to find a girl for her brother from California. Today, he is also in the United States and lives with his family close to Laila. She is very happy that her brother is also in the United States. She hopes that one day her family can also move to the United States.

Laila believed that the political turmoil in the last three decades has caused so much trouble for the Afghan people. She thought many men, women, and children spend their lives in misery in Afghanistan. People need food, water, shelter, and peace. Education, work, happiness, and other things come next, she thought. According to her, all the problems of illiteracy, war, corruption, and other problems are because of poverty. She hoped that the Afghan government and with the help of the international community could bring peace to the country and provide jobs for people as soon as possible so that people could find food and shelter.

SUMMARY

Almost all the participants came from a background that defined their narratives and immigration to the United States. They all came from families that suffered somehow during the political crises in Afghanistan in the last three decades. Some had bitter experiences from the Communist era, and some from the Mujahideen and the Taliban regimes. Almost all of the participants had their own narratives about why they married the Afghan American men and how they experienced life in the United States.

The women were all very young when they got married and their husbands were older than them; some husbands were much older. The engagement parties, *shab-e-khina*, and the weddings the women had, involved various cultural traditions, particularly in regard to how many people were invited, where the wedding was held, and so forth. In addition, some sort of monetary issue under various names such as, *jawab-e-shirini, gala, toyana, mahr, shirbaha,* and so forth were part of the marriage.

The interviews also showed that most participants in the study had some sort of employment, either part time or full time. Some were housewives, whereas others seemed successful in their educational goals and careers. Most of them had a major appreciation for the value of education. They have either had their own interests and zeal in continuing their education or it has been their families and husbands who strived for their success as well.

Some of the participants faced various challenges but in most aspects they seemed to have found happy, comfortable, and economically independent lives. The most telling challenge was loneliness and lack of interaction in the first few months until they found friends and overcame the culture shock. Some also had other reasons such as their children and how they should train them and what kind of education they should receive. Some worried about their jobs because of the recession. A few also worried about their immediate families who are still left behind in Afghanistan.

Nevertheless, almost all of the participants mentioned how happy they were with their life experience in the United States. They all believed that they were luckier than most women back in Afghanistan. They insisted on the importance of employment, education, freedom, peace, human rights, security, and the like. In addition, the most important thing they first realized in the United States was the facilities such as gas, water, cleanliness as well as security, peace, human rights, and so forth.

There were some important issues such as domination, subjugation, freedom, economic dependence or independence, marriage traditions, consanguineous marriages, monetary issues, how the couples met each other and so forth. These need further analysis and most of these concepts came up in the interviews that will be discussed in detail as themes derived from the participants' interviews.

Chapter 5

DISCUSSION

DISCUSSION OF THEMES

Many themes appeared from the interviews. Although each participant in the study had a unique narrative, still many similar ideas were expressed. No doubt, the interviews revealed characteristics and patterns previously discovered by other researchers. The women, who immigrated to the United States by means of marriage to Afghan American men, have all faced the realities of life before and after their immigration to the United States. The themes emerging from the interviews also provide a significant amount of support to answers to the research questions and are discussed in detail as follows:

A BITTER PAST

Each participant and her family had the courage to survive through extreme hardship and war trauma, particularly during the last three decades of socio-political crises in Afghanistan. The participants were all somehow affected by either the Communist regime, the Mujahideen or the Taliban. Years of hunger, oppression, deprivations, illiteracy, migration, and lack of freedom has made Afghans suffer the most. Particularly during the 1990s, the Afghan women were direct victims under the Mujahideen and the Taliban regimes. Almost all of the participants and their families were either a direct or indirect victim of the changing situation in the last three decades in Afghanistan.

All the participants were displaced and forced to abandon their homes during the crises in the last three decades. Some left one city and moved to the other; however, four of the participants stated that they left the country. Families tried to escape from Afghanistan to a safer place however possible in order to protect their women from the regimes, particularly the Taliban. The immigration took place in millions in order to find a secure and a safer environment.

Although life in Diaspora, particularly in Pakistan and Iran, has been fruitful for Afghan refugees, some have bitter stories of how hard life was for them away from their homeland. Nadia's family found the opportunity to immigrate to Quetta, a city in Pakistan, and Zohal's family to Peshawar, another city in Pakistan. Also, Nahid's family moved to the city of Dushanbe in Tajikistan, and Laila's family immigrated to Iran. The main goal of immigration to these countries for the participants was to escape from violence, war, and in order to seek educational and job opportunities, particularly for the women.

A HAPPY LIFE IN THE UNITED STATES

Most of the participants agreed that they were satisfied with life in the United States for various reasons. When the participants first came to the United States, they liked the comfort and facilities that they did not enjoy or enjoy as much in Afghanistan. Almost all of them compared their lives to how hard it was in Afghanistan, and how comfortable they are in the United States at the present time. They emphasized the enjoyment of the basic human needs such as warm and cold water, washing and drying machines, gas, 24-hour electricity, cleanliness, clean air, less pollution and other privileges that meant a lot to them.

In addition, most of the women believed that job opportunity in the United States is an enormous privilege to everybody. Some thought both men and women can build their skills, get educated, and enter the job market with no major challenges. Almost all of the participants said they were happy that they had jobs or their husbands had decent jobs.

Most importantly, all the participants placed emphasis on the peace, rule of law, and security in the United States. Memories of war from Afghanistan have remained with the Afghan immigrants and might never be forgotten. Experiences of not being able to leave home because of war, torture, and fear of being killed were issues that each participant reiterated on and remembered. Now, living a life with no fear of bullets or bombs in the United States is what has brought peace of mind to each Afghan immigrant. Most participants thought financial stability, education, success, and happiness was related to peace and peace was the most important privilege for them in the host nation.

In fact, all the participants felt lucky to have come to the United States. They generally thought they would have been left uneducated and ignorant if they stayed in Afghanistan. Here they believe they have all the opportunities that they did not have in Afghanistan. Particularly, educational opportunities were of the highest importance to the Afghan women.

FREEDOM

Although no specific question was asked about freedom, the participants talked about it either directly or indirectly. Their perceptions about freedom varied. Most of the participants stressed education and employment as freedom and success. Getting educated and entering the workforce was the only way for freedom and their independence, they thought. This can also relate to Gilman's theory where she considered women's freedom as their earning and economical self sufficiency (Appelrouth and Idles, 2008).

The participants repeatedly stated that Afghan women do not have freedom in Afghanistan because they are mostly uneducated and unskilled, and also because they do not work. That is why they suffer from poverty and are solely dependent on men for food, clothing, shelter, and so forth. The participants, however, suggested solutions to the reasons why women were kept uneducated and unemployed. They emphasized the importance of education and work for Afghan women.

The participants spoke of the significance of the consequences of war for approximately thirty years that confined Afghan women at home. During the war, families were scared about sending their daughters to schools and working environments. Their girls could get shot, raped, kidnapped, and even trafficked. Almost every participant mentioned the Taliban regime and their cruelty to women, particularly how the Taliban closed the schools and work opportunities for them. Some participants also believed it was their traditionalist men, particularly fathers who did not allow women to study and work. In addition, some participants thought there is much unemployment in Afghanistan and there are jobs neither for men nor for women.

Nadia and Nahid had got their bachelor's degrees and they both worked at the time of the study. To them freedom was education and work. They thought if women do not work, they are not free. Sarah too had an associate degree and was working as a receptionist. She too, thought women in America work as men and that is good. Sarah thought education was the "key to success." She enjoyed volunteering for non-governmental organizations who worked for the Afghan women. Sarah thought education should be made compulsory for all the Afghan women so that no woman is left behind uneducated. In addition, she insisted that families should not be "allowed to deprive" their daughters of going to schools and spreading education.

Farida had her own business of hair dressing. She made money, and thought she enjoyed freedom and independence in the United States. To her, freedom also meant "doing anything a person wants which is not against the law." She thought marriage, divorce, and working rights are what the United States government has given to both men and women. During the Taliban regime she thought women did not have any rights under the government laws. But in the United States freedom is good.

Laila's case was very interesting. She had broken an engagement with her fiancé, who was also one of her distant relatives. The reason why she broke the engagement was because he wanted her to stop going to the university. Laila chose to have freedom and continue her education. Her family was happy too that she broke her engagement. They thought Hamid, who was from the United States and proposed to Laila, would support her with her future goals. Here in the United States, Laila still continued to pursue her education and Hamid supported her. Freedom meant a lot to Laila and her family.

The schools were closed for women in Afghanistan for almost a decade. Life became unbearable for some families who saw their teenage daughters deprived of going to school. Some of the participants continued to read some story books at home, or their parents helped them continue reading and writing. They hoped to see their daughters get educated in Pakistan, Iran, Tajikistan, or in other countries. That is how Afghans immigrated to other countries, particularly the neighboring countries of Iran and Pakistan, in hope of having basic human freedoms.

CHALLENGES

The newly immigrant participants faced many challenges such as culture shock, depression, homesickness, loneliness, sense of being an alien, and difficulty adapting to society and so forth particularly in the first few months. Later, life became more interesting for most. Almost every participant had a hard time and faced at least one of the above-mentioned challenges. Some like Zohal still suffer after years but most of the participants have overcome the challenges the faced.

Coming to the United States of America from a third world war-torn country like Afghanistan can be a great culture shock. The women who first came to the United States lost almost everybody with whom they had a connection. Everything, including food, shops, streets, houses, people, and so forth was strange to them. They had very little or no familiarity with even the ordinary things such as shopping, interacting, educational system, driving, and so forth.

The common interaction with family and relatives that Afghans enjoy in Afghanistan became limited for the participants in the United States. Major festivals and occasions, such as *Eid* and *Nawroz,* mean a lot to Afghans, but in the United States these occasions and festivals are barely celebrated. Women in particular drink tea and talk with other women daily but almost every adult man and woman works in the United States and they do not have much time for interaction.

When the newly immigrant women first come to United States, they realize how busy everybody is. There are not a lot of women, including family and relatives, and even neighbors do not have much time to interact with these women. Going to Afghanistan is hard and costly. Most participants said they interact with their family and friends through phone calls every week or every other week.

Some participants, such as Frishta, had only visited her family back in Afghanistan twice in the last nine years. Sarah has been visiting her family every year but she still thinks life would be much better if they were with her in the United States. Zohal, for example, stated that life for her is "meaningless" without having her family and relatives around her. Frishta thinks about her family all the time and this is what always bothers her the most. She said she was always worried about her family's safety and well being back in Afghanistan, and missed them a lot. That is how each participant mentioned lack of interaction as a major challenge that caused loneliness and depression when they first came to the United States.

Adaptation to the new host country is a major challenge for the participants. Lack of English language skills made it extremely hard for some of them to communicate and find friends during the first year or two of their immigration. Some spoke English when they immigrated and therefore did not face a lot of challenges. Frishta thought transportation was a problem for her because she did not speak the language. She found it hard to use a bus to get to the supermarket or to the home of a friend or relative. She got her driver's license after seven years. However, although Zohal thought adaptation was not hard in the United States, she still missed the interaction she had back in Afghanistan.

Farida talked about enjoying theme parks, beaches, and other recreation sites in California that made her happy and enjoy life in America. To Maria, her children's Islamic training was important. She was worried about her children when she first came to California. Later, as she was able to send her children to Orange County Islamic educational centers, she felt much better and happy with her life in America. In addition, Maria was worried about the influence of gangs, drugs, premarital sex, and that her children do not get misguided.

A major challenge for Laila was traveling by herself and facing a new life filled with culture shock. Meeting new people and places was something inconceivable for Laila. She said she was not able to think properly for days and even weeks before things returned to normal. Laila found a girl for her brother who was in Kabul, and now he is also in America and lives close to her. She hopes to get her family in the United States one day too.

In short, most of the participants said they did not face major challenges in the United States. The comfortable life meant a lot to them. There was no worry about their safety and freedom. They enjoyed the weather, their jobs, and families. However, still the participants in this study experienced loneliness and lack of social interaction in the Unites States as compared to Afghanistan.

TRADITIONAL KHASTGARI AND MARRIAGE

The Afghan immigrant women generally described their marriages as traditional as practiced in Afghanistan. Mostly, it was the man's parents or sisters who went for *khastgari* to Afghanistan for their son's future wife. Sometimes, like in Frishta's case, the man went also to see the girl or for the engagement and marriage events. Nadia was in Quetta, Pakistan, when her *khastgars* proposed to her.

Interestingly, Sarah's *khastgars* first sent her the photos of Ali, her future husband, and proposed to her through Ali's cousin. After a week, when Ali's family got the preapproval answer from Sarah's family, they went to Kabul for the official proposal. Thus, marriage proposals were not undertaken by individuals themselves and the *khastgari* took place.

Usually *khastgari* takes weeks, and even months, and an average of five times before the girls' families agree to the proposal. However, it is concluded with a positive answer in the very first or second *khastgari* when the proposing groom comes from the United States. That is usually the sign of good luck when a girl finds a *khastgar* from the United States in particular. Almost all male counterparts had come to the United States during the last thirty years. The condition that seemed very important for families for *khastgari* included taking their daughter to the United States after marriage, and potentially her brothers, or even the rest of the girl's family.

CONSANGUINITY AND THE MALE COUNTERPART

The interviews revealed that participants mostly had consanguineous marriages in addition to the common traditional arranged marriages. Tribal, religious, linguistic, and familial ties were all part of the marriages that the participants described. Almost all the participants except Laila were somehow related to the men they married. Frishta and Maria, for example, married their father's cousins, Nadia her cousin's brother-in-law, Zohal her mother's relative, and Farida married her second cousin. Also Sarah's husband was her cousin's husband's relative. Nahid's husband was her father's distant relative. Only Laila was not related to her husband at all.

Consanguineous marriages are still very prevalent based on familial, religious, linguistic, and tribal ties in Afghanistan. Even for Laila, although she married somebody who was not related to her, her husband was from her ethnic group and same religious sect. The *khastgari* process also happens easily because of the previous connections and contact that the two families have had together.

Little Or No Contact Prior to Marriage

All of the participants had arranged marriages. It was not a direct connection that the girl started with her potential husband before marriage. The participants basically did not know each other very well. Only Nahid knew her husband for a few years. Others married their husbands with no or little prior connections. The only time they got to know each other was after *khastgari* and then only for a few weeks or months. Nadia and Frishta, for example, actually saw their husbands for the first time on the day of the engagement. Also, the age of the participants' husbands was remarkable. Age variations started from five years in the case of Zohal's husband to sixteen years like Nadia's husband.

Maria's case was interesting and showed much of her own authority in her marriage decision. She was in contact with her future husband through email and phone before marriage. Her husband Navid had already been married once and had a teenage son from a Swedish woman. Maria chose to marry Navid after talking to him. She described it as her own decision because she thought her life would be good in the United States as well as because Navid was not a "stranger." They were relatives.

Also Nahid knew Jawad for years. They had been refugees in Pakistan and lived close to each other's home. Nahid did not give any detail of her relationship to Jawad in Pakistan, but she was happy that Jawad proposed to her. Thus, the way most participants described their relationship with their *khastgars* was that they had little or no prior contact with them.

Monetary Gifts

Almost all participants talked about some sort of monetary gifts that her family received from the proposing family. Now two things have to be differentiated. First, Mahr is usually not given to the family during marriage. It is promised to be given to the girl if the couple goes through divorce in the future. However, *gula, toyana, walwar, shirbaha,* and *jawab-e-shirini* do not have religious legitimacy and they are basic traditional practice. Although most of the marriages were consanguine-ous, participants confirmed that their families received monetary gifts from the groom's family. Frishta's family received $10,000 as *gala*. Na-dia's *mahr* and *shirbaha* was $12,000. Zohal's *toyana* was $6,000. Farid's *jawab-e-shirini* was $10,000. Sarah's *jawab-e-shirini* was $2,500, and her *shirbaha* was $6,000. Maria's family received $4,000 for *shirbaha*. Nahid's family received $4,000 as *jawab-e-shirini*. In addition, families received monetary and material gifts for the engagement and wedding parties.

As described, the money was usually given to the families in the Afghani currency. The participants did not emphasize on whether their families asked for the money or whether the proposing man offered it voluntarily. *Jawab-e-shirini* is usually given voluntarily by the man. However, *gala, shirbaha, walwar,* and *toyana* are gifts that the bride's family requires the man to pay.

BACKBREAKING WEDDING COSTS

One thing that was very prevalent was the expensive weddings that the participants had in general. In addition to monetary gifts, the jewelry, bride dress, groom suit or traditional clothes, dress for close relatives for both the groom and bride's family, gifts for *shahbala*, dinner for hun-dreds of guests in wedding halls or restaurants, musical band for guests' entertainment, decorated vehicles for transportation of the bride and groom, the guests, and so forth seem very costly for an average Afghan to be able to provide to the girl's family.

It has become a common practice that the girl's family requires the wedding to be celebrated in a wedding hall. Now in Afghanistan, the number of guests people invite to a common wedding party reaches hundreds. Almost every participant had her wedding party held at a wedding hall. Each, except in Nadia's case, had invited hundreds of people in her engagement and wedding parties. In addition, there is the engagement, *shab-e-khina,* and *takht jami* ceremonies where at least fifty people are invited.

The bride-price and other expenses above seem backbreaking and almost impossible for the average Afghan to provide. That is why so many men in their 30s remain single. Approximately $10,000-$30,000 dollars was spent on the participants' marriages including everything. That probably is not backbreaking for an Afghan American man who works and might save that money in the United States in a matter of a year or two. But, the average Afghan man earns 30 dollars a month, and works his entire life to afford his wedding costs and his bride-price demanded by the girl's family.

Here, families who are traditional and less "open-minded" demand so much for their daughters. They will be hoping for somebody to come from *kharej* (a foreign country) to propose to their daughters. As a consequence girls in these families will be left unmarried until their late 20s and early 30s, which is not common in Afghanistan. The same thing will happen to some men in Afghanistan where they will not be able to afford the marriage. In short, the monetary incentives offered or provided by the man from *kharej* will bring him the young beautiful girl that he wants although he might be uneducated or middle aged.

COMPARING ONESELF TO AFGHAN AND AMERICAN WOMEN

Almost all the participants felt luckier than the women in Afghanistan for various reasons. The participants were conscious of the more privileges they had compared to women in Afghanistan. First of all, comfort is something that the participants believed they have in the United States, whereas most women in Afghanistan experience poverty. Second, it was suffering because of the war and harassment because of the Taliban in rural areas. Finally, the women described patriarchal traditions that harm women in Afghanistan.

The participants gave examples such as washing clothes and dishes, cooking, cleaning, and so forth that were hard and uncomfortable for Afghan women due to lack of facilities such as water, gas, and electricity. However, doing the house chores in the United States for women is very easy and comfortable. Participants stressed poverty and believed most families suffer from it. A lot of people do not live in decent houses. They can not afford to buy washing machines or a power generator for electricity. It is hard for them to afford water boilers for bathrooms and kitchens. Women who can afford gas use it for cooking but a large number still use coal or wood for cooking and warming water for bathing. It is hard to provide basic needs, the participants thought. However, life is not that hard even for poor families here in the United States, they thought.

The participants also expressed their feelings that historically, particularly during the civil war and the Taliban regimes, women were hurt the most. Even today women are harassed and threatened by the Taliban in rural areas. Families are scared of sending their daughters to schools. The participants thought they have more security in America than the women in Afghanistan. Women go to school in America and nobody has the right to deprive them of going to school. They thought the law enforcement protects them from harassment.

Also, the participants stated that some women are victims of control and patriarchy by their brothers and parents who disallow them to go to school or work. The participants thought their freedoms were important. They described their husbands as more egalitarian husbands than some male counterparts in Afghanistan. Some participants suggested that the government laws should be made compulsory for women's education. She added that men in the family should not be allowed to stop women from going to school.

The women in the study believed a large number of women are still victims of control by the society, particularly some social norms that encourage them to stay home and not spread education. For example, encouraging women to be housewives is very common in Afghanistan among traditionalists. Some of the participants thought most uneducated men in Afghanistan expect their wives to stay home, cook, clean, and take care of the children. The mentality of those men is that the role of man food and shelter provider for the family but the woman should stay home.

Most importantly, the participants thought it is also the opinion of some women who believe it is not appropriate for them to work outside. They believe it is their husbands' responsibility to work and provide food for the family. They feel that their most important job is to stay home, take care of the children, and provide them with good training. Some women also think that doing house chores is their responsibility not a man's. However, some participants believed that only being a housewife and taking care of the children is not good for women. They suggested that women get educated and work even if part-time. Women should work, earn their own living, and enjoy freedom.

The women in the study felt that they face no subjugation or control by neither the government nor their male counterparts and families in the United States. They generally thought they acculturated and adapted well into American society socially and economically. For them, freedom meant their economical independency and as well as education. They thought both job and educational opportunities are available in the United States, and thus they thought they enjoyed freedom.

Nevertheless, one of the participants in the study described herself as family oriented. Frishta thought she was family oriented unlike most other American women. She thought it is better for women who have children to stay home and not work. She thought she would never leave her children with a babysitter. Also, she thought not all women should necessarily work outside of the home. It is better for women to stay home and men to work. In Frishta's case, probably it was because she was not working. She was deprived of going to school after reaching the 8th grade. She basically did not have any skills except being a stay-at-home mom. However, other participants thought there were a lot of facilities and comfort; cooking, cleaning, and taking care of the children, is easier in America than it was in Afghanistan. In addition to doing house chores, they emphasized the significance of working and getting more educated.

CITIZENSHIP

Citizenship was considered a privilege by most participants. Citizenship obviously helps people sponsor their other family members to come to the Unite States from any corner of the world. It takes six months to three years for newly married men and women to get their citizenship when they are married to an American citizen. It also requires a citizenship test. However, looking at the participants' interviews, it seemed like some have been in the United States for almost a decade but have not become a citizen yet. Basically, only two of the participants, Nadia and Farida, had gotten their citizenship and others were still green card holders.

For Frishta, who has been in the United States since 2000, the reason for not having gotten her citizenship was lack of English language skills, and also traveling out of the country twice. Zohal immigrated to the United States in 2005 and had her green card. As in her interview, she seemed to be still suffering from loneliness and depression. She hoped to go and live in Afghanistan with her husband. That might be the reason why she did not apply for citizenship. Sarah is not a citizen yet either, and she has been in California since 1999. She thought "school, work, and raising children" has kept her from getting her citizenship. However, she was hopeful to get it soon.

Also, Nahid was not a citizen either. She immigrated in 2004. She did not hope for her parents to come to the United States. Her parents thought they had a happy life in Kabul. As a result, citizenship did not seem very essential to Nahid. Maria also immigrated in 2000 and was a green card holder. She seemed like a very busy woman. She was raising three children and was pregnant at the time of the interview. That might have been a reason for her citizenship delay. Laila has a green card and will get her citizenship next year. She did not seem to have a major problem with her language skills since she got her Bachelor's degree from the United States. Thus, these were some of the various reasons why the participants did not get their citizenship.

CONCLUSIONS

This exploratory study was a case study of the eight Afghan women who immigrated to the United States through marriage to the Afghan American men. Through this qualitative research method, in-depth, and face to face interviews with the participants, the goal of this research was to explore their experiences of Afghan women in America. The feminist theoretical approach further helped in analyzing whether the marriages of these women to Afghan American men were subject to domination and subjugation, or freedom and economical independence.

When common mail-order brides, advertized on catalogues or websites, were compared to Afghan immigrant women, both similarities and differences were observed in terms of how they experience life. The Afghan immigrant women in the study, however, were not advertised in magazines or websites. Like mail-order brides, the Afghan women usually came from impoverished families. They looked for educated, economically stable, and more egalitarian Afghan men who lived in the United States. These women usually showed less interest in the age of their future husbands who were much older than them. They mostly aimed for equality, freedom, educational, and economical opportunities. Thus, these were some similarities that the Afghan women had with common mail-order brides.

Also, immigrating Afghan women reported more issues than those associated with the phenomenon of mail-order brides. These types of marriage arrangements include consanguinity, tribal, ethnic, and linguistic affiliations between couples. The Afghan immigrant women predominantly get married to Afghan American men. The marriages traditionally involve monetary issues as the participants reported such as *mahr, shirbaha, gala, toyana, jawab-e-shirini,* and so forth. In addition, Afghan American men, who marry their brides from Afghanistan, usually offer (or the bride family demands) expensive wedding gifts, jewelry, and wedding celebrations in halls that cost thousands of dollars for the reception of hundreds of guests. Material exchanges of land and livestock were not reported in the study, though. Neither was the issue of bride exchanges between tribes reported.

The participants openly spoke about their subjective experiences in the United States. Almost all the women in the study reported the political turmoil and war under the Communists, the Mujahideen, and the Taliban regimes in the last three decades had major effects on Afghan women's lives. They also reported the crises as a leading factor why they preferred to marry an Afghan American man and immigrate to the United States. They were direct victims of war and despotism particularly during the Mujahideen and the Taliban regimes when basic human rights were snatched from them. Most of them had gone through poverty along with their families. They were deprived of their basic rights of working and going to school. They had similar stories of a tragic past that lead them to choose to marry their current husbands.

By most, life in America was reported as a gift. While the women lived in Afghanistan, they described their lives with lots of hardship. Most of the families suffered from lack of infrastructure, educational and employment opportunities, and poverty. However, life in America has brought them more peace of mind, comfort, better educational and employment opportunities, and, most importantly, freedom and independence.

The challenges the women reported were significant. Particularly in the first year or so, culture shock, depression, and loneliness were reported because of lack of interaction with family and friends. Participants also commented that transportation problems, and more importantly lack of English language skills, were major issues to deal with. These challenges were mentioned as temporary for most participants. Later, they found more friends and relatives that helped them cope up with their loneliness. Continuing their education and having a job were major factors in overcoming the challenges they faced and helped in their adaptation and assimilation into the mainstream culture in the United States.

Today, after Afghanistan's transition to a democratic society, the international community's focus is on the liberation of Afghan women and their capacity building through building more educational institutions. Afghan women, too, see their freedom and independence in employment and education. There are still challenges that Afghan women are facing in the Afghan society because of the traditionalists and how they interpret Islamic Shariya laws for women. The Ministry of Women's Affairs and some Afghan feminists have been working on advocacy programs for women through the support of the United Nations, Human Rights Commission, and other non-governmental organizations. In spite of all that, the immigration of Afghan women and their marriage to Afghan American men is continuing for various reasons.

Recommendations for Future Research

The identity of the researcher as an "Afghan male researcher" interviewing the Afghan women about their Afghan male counterparts was always worrisome. The worry was that the participants might think of the researcher as just another traditional Afghan man and might not share everything. Prior to the interviews, the participants were curious about who the researcher was and what this research would be used for and why the researcher was conducting this research. Knowing that he was a sociology student at California State University, Fullerton, and that he would use the interviews only for academic purposes, probably was a help but the fear of not getting enough information always existed.

For a study like this one, it would be much better that an Afghan woman conduct the interviews. Although the Afghan women openly discussed their circumstances, they mostly talked about how happy their lives were in the United States. The challenges they mentioned were only for the first few months or a year or two and they were basic issues unrelated to domination, subjugation, and abuse. When asked about their marriages, they mostly tended to show happiness and satisfaction with their husbands. There was no abuse, domination, control or subjugation reported. Probably an Afghan female researcher will get more information from these women if and how they are facing subjugation in their marriage. The participants will probably get more personal with a female researcher and tell her about the dilemmas or problems they are facing with their male counterparts.

Appendix

Appendix 1

QUESTIONNAIRE FOR THE INTERVIEWS

INTERVIEW QUESTIONS

The interviews will be conducted in Persian (Farsi-Dari). The participants will answer open-ended questions. The questions will be simple worded, and will include the following:

DEMOGRAPHIC QUESTIONS:

1. How old are you?
2. Education level?
3. Occupation?

INTERVIEW QUESTIONS

1. Tell me about your family? (Father, mother, brothers, sisters and their occupations, and where they live)
2. Tell me about your family in the US? (Husband, children and others in the family and their occupations)?
3. How did you meet your husband?

4. Describe your wedding? (Where and how you got married? Was there any monetary issue involved?)
5. Tell me about how you are experiencing life in the United States?
6. What are the things you like most about your experience in the United States?
7. What are the things you do not like about your experience in the United States?
8. What major challenges do you face in America (In family and at work)?
9. What was your perception of the United States while in Afghanistan before moving to the United States? And what difference did you find than expected?
10. How did you perceive American women before you immigrated to the US? What do you think of them now?
11. How many times have you been married? Is your current husband your first spouse?
12. Did you ask your father or mother about your husband/somebody you wanted to marry?
13. Were you in contact with somebody/your husband before you married him?
14. Did you ask your husband in the US to call your parents and ask them about marrying you?
15. How do you compare yourself to Afghan women in Afghanistan and American women here in California?

Appendix 2

CONSENT FORM

Hello. My name is Sayid Sattar Langary. I am a graduate student in the Sociology Department at California State University, Fullerton.

I am conducting this research for my thesis. The study is about the life experiences of Afghan women who have immigrated to the United States through marriage. I am asking you to participate in an in-depth face to face interview with me. The interview might take between 45-90 minutes of your time. I ask you to answer the questions to the best of your abilities.

Your participation is voluntary. If you choose not to participate or withdraw from participation at anytime, you can. If you skip or refuse to answer a question, you can. This research is confidential to the extent allowed by law. You don't need to give your exact name, address or other people's names. To assure you of the confidentiality, the results of this study might be published but will not include any names, address or any kind of identification information. The interviews will be digitally recorded. The data will be kept in a locked desk until the interviews are transcribed in a word processing file on computer. Only the researcher and Dr. Joseph Weber –the supervisor of the study will have access to the data. After the interviews are transcribed, the audio file will be deleted permanently on August 30th.

The research is for exploratory purposes only. No business or financial conflict of interest relates to results of this study. There would be no monetary or material benefit for your participation in this study. However, the summary of research findings or a copy of the research paper could be given to you once done. Your participation is very valuable in the study and it will improve further understanding of the experience of Afghan women in California.

Please contact me or Dr. Joseph Weber if you have any questions at:

Sayid Sattar Langary: sattarlangary@csu.fullerton.edu or Cell: 760.803.9070

Dr. Joseph Weber: jweber@exchange.fullerton.edu

I have carefully read this consent form and understand it. I confirm that I am 18+ years old and agree to participate in this study.

Participant name: _____

Signature: _____

Date: _____

BIBLIOGRAPHY

Anderson, M. J. (1993). A license to abuse: The impact of conditional status on female immigrants. *The Yale Law Journal 10*(6), 1401–1430. Retrieved from Sociological Abstracts database.

Appelrouth, Scott, Laura Desfor Edles. (2008). *Classical and contemporary sociological theory: Text and readings:* Pine Forge Press. California State University, Northridge.

Aseel, M. Q. (2003). *Torn between cultures: An Afghan American woman speaks out.* Sterling, Virginia: Capital Books Inc.

Babbie, E. (2006). *The practice of social research*: 11th edition. Thomson Wadsworth.

Barrenburg, J. 2003. Beyond kinship algebra: Values and the riddle of Pashtun marriage structure. *Institut fur ethnologie, Dietrich Reimer Verlag*; Berlin, *128*(2), 269-292. Retrieved from Sociological Abstracts database.

Buss, D. M., Todd K.S., Lee A. K., & Randy J. L. (2001). A half century of American mate preferences. *Journal of marriage and the family, 63*(2), 491-503.

Clark, J. (2004). Filipino women in Tasmania: Negotiating gender ideologies. *Asian and Pacific Migration Journal, 13*(3), 363-380.

Dupree, Nancy H. (1998). Afghan women under the Taliban. In William Maley (Ed.), *Fundamentalism reborn?: Afghanistan and the Taliban* (pp. 145–166). London: Hurst and Co.

Dupree, Nancy H. (2002). The family during crisis in Afghanistan. *Journal of Comparative Family Studies, 1*(1), 311-331.

Eng L. D. (2006). Political economics of passion: Studies in gender and sexuality, transnational adoption and global woman. *Roundtable on Global Woman, 1*(7), 49-59.

Fazel, Solaiman (2009). Afghan Immigration to the United States, 1979-2009: The Westward Movement, ed. G. M. Bakken, Facts on File, Inc., (2009 forthcoming).

Felicity, Schaeffer.G. (2006). Planet-Love.com: Cyber brides in the Americas and the transnational routes of U.S. masculinity. *Journal of Women in Culture and Society, 31*(2), 331-356.

Ghobar, M.G.M. (2002). *Afghanistan dar Massir Tarikh* (Afghanistan in the course of history). Persian Text. Reprinted. Peshawar, Pakistan: Maiwand Publications.

Hesse-Biber, S. N., & Patricia, L. (2005). *The practice of qualitative research:* Sage Publications. Thousand Oaks, London, New Delhi.

Hochschild, A. R. (2002). Love and gold: in *Global Woman: Nannies, Maids, and Sex Workers in the New Economy*, ed. B. Ehrenreich & A.Hochschild. New York: Metropolitan Books.

Hooper, C. (2001). *Manly states: Masculinities, international relations, and gender politics.* New York: Columbia University Press.

Johnson, E. (2007). *Dreaming of a mail-order husband: Russian-American internet romance.* Duke University Press: Durham and London.

Kandiyoti, D. (2007). Old dilemmas or new challenges? The politics of gender and reconstruction in Afghanistan. *Development and Change, 38*(2): 169–199.

Kojima,Y. (2001). In the business of cultural reproduction: Theoretical implications of the mail-order bride phenomenon. *Women's Studies International Forum, 24*(2), 199-209.

Langevin, L., & Marie-Claire, B. (2000). *Trafficking in women in Canada: A critical analysis of the legal framework governing immigrant live-in caregivers and mail-order brides*: Canada.

Lee, H. (2008). International marriage and the state in South Korea: Focusing on governmental policy. *Citizenship Studies, 12*(1), 107-123.

Lipson, J. G., & Omidian, Patricia A. (1996). *Refugees in America in the 1990s: A reference handbook,* Westport, Conn: Greenwood Press.

Miller, E.K. (2006). The Afghan Symptom Checklist: A Culturally Grounded Approach to Mental Health Assessment in a Conflict Zone. *American Journal of Orthopsychiatry, 76*(4), 423–433.

Minervini, B. P., & Francis, T. M. (2006). The mating strategies and mate preferences of mail-order brides. *Cross-Cultural Research, 40*(2), 111-129.

Moghadam M. V. (2002). Patriarchy, the Taliban, and politics of public space in Afghanistan. *Women's Studies International Forum, 25*(1), 19–31.

Narayan, R. K. (2000). *The Mahabharata: A shortened modern prose version of the Indian epic*, Chicago, IL: University of Chicago Press.

Pawlowski, B., & Slawomir, K. (2002). The impact of traits offered in personal advertisements on response rates. *Evolution and Human Behavior, 23*(2), 139-149.

Rashid, Ahmed (2000). Taliban: *Militant Islam, oil, and fundamentalism in Central Asia.* New Haven: Yale University Press.

Sadat, M. H. (2006). The Afghan experience: An exploratory study of societal realities through the lenses of Afghan diasporic literary works. Claremont Graduate University and San Diego State University.

Sadat, M. H. (2008). Hyphenating *Afghaniyat* (Afghan-ness) in the Afghan Diaspora. *Journal of Muslim Minority Affairs, 28*(3), 329-342. Retrieved from Sociological Abstracts Database.

Stake, R. E. (1995). *The art of case study research.* Thousand Oaks, CA: Sage.

Wahab, A., Ahmad, M., & Shah, S.A. (2005). Migration as a determinant of marriage pattern: Preliminary report on consanguinity among Afghans. *Journal of Biosocial Science, 38*(3), 315-325. Cambridge University Press. Retrieved from Sociological Abstracts Database.

Winthrop, R. (2003). Reflections on working in post-conflict Afghanistan: Local versus international perspectives on gender relations. *Women's Studies Quarterly, 3*(4) GenderWatch (GW), 247- 252.